Ruach

The Space and Grace for Hope and Healing, and Wholeness

Table of Contents

Dedication

I want to give glory first and foremost to Jesus Christ, My Healer, Redeemer, and Restorer.

To my loving husband, Gerald— Honey, you sacrifice every day for me and the kids. You continuously show me what true, unconditional love looks like. You embody the love of Christ, and I am so deeply grateful for you. There are not enough words to express how much you mean to me. You have played a major role in my healing. Because of your love, I felt safe enough to be vulnerable. You gave me both the space and the grace to heal on my own terms and in my own way. I love you beyond words. I love you beyond time.

To my children — You are my greatest gifts. Each of you carries a light that has brightened my darkest days. Your laughter, strength, and love remind me daily of God's faithfulness. Watching you grow has healed places in me I didn't know were broken. Thank you for loving me through my becoming. I'm honored to be your mother.

To my mother —Thank you for being my first intercessor, my spiritual mentor, and my unwavering support. Your walk with God shaped mine. Your strength, wisdom, and prayers have carried me through more than you know. You are one of my life's greatest blessings.

Thank you to all my family and friends who encouraged me when my own healing journey felt long and heavy. Thank you to the women and men who bravely pursue healing; your courage inspired every word of this book. And to every reader: thank you for trusting me to walk beside you for a few sacred steps of your journey. May the God of Hope fill you with all joy and peace as you trust in Him (Romans 15:13).

6

Scripture Theme

"And now these three remain: faith, hope, and love. But the greatest of these is love." — 1 Corinthians 13:13 (NIV)

"For I will restore health to you and heal you of your wounds," says the Lord. — Jeremiah 30:17 (NKJV)

"The thief comes only to steal and kill and destroy; I have come that they may have life, and have it to the full." — John 10:10 (NIV)

Introduction
Ruach
The Breath That Awakens

Before you turn another page, I want you to pause and hear this:

You are seen.
You are loved.
You are not forgotten.

This book was not written to impress you. It was breathed out to impact you. Every word, every reflection, and every truth you will encounter was first soaked in prayer and breathed on by the Spirit of the living God. In Hebrew, the word *Ruach* means breath, wind, or Spirit. It is not just a poetic symbol. It is the very essence of God moving upon the earth and within us. It is His breath that hovered over the deep in Genesis 1:2, bringing order to chaos. It was His breath that filled Adam's lifeless form and made him a living being (Genesis 2:7). It was His breath that came upon the valley of dry bones in Ezekiel 37, causing what was once dead to rise again.

The Ruach of God still moves today. It moves not only over creation but within the hidden places of our hearts, the places we don't often show others. It is the breath that revives, restores, and resurrects. This same Ruach breath will meet you on the pages ahead.

There may be moments while reading this book where you feel exposed, vulnerable, or even overwhelmed. Don't run from it. Lean in. Take a deep breath. Let the Ruach blow over your weary soul. Let it bring peace to your inner chaos. Let it awaken hope where you've buried it and speak life where you thought it was too late. As you journey through the three parts: Hope, Healing, and Wholeness, know this. God has breathed on every page. This book is not just ink and paper. It is a holy invitation to encounter the breath of God in personal, intimate ways.

This is more than a book. It is a tool. A companion. A guide for the moments you don't have words, for the days when your soul aches more than your body, and for the nights when all you can do is weep.

This is not just for this season of your life. It is for every season to come.

Let me tell you plainly. There is no shame in needing hope. There is no guilt in needing healing. And there is certainly no weakness in desiring wholeness. As you walk through these pages, may the Ruach of God blow gently but powerfully upon you.

But here is the part I don't want you to miss. This journey isn't just for you.

In the end, the goal is not only that you find healing but that you become a vessel of it. We were never designed to do life alone. We were created for community, for restoration, and for divine purpose. I pray that you would turn back and find someone who is stuck, lost, or broken just like you once were and that you would bring them with you. You do not need permission to snatch souls out of darkness. Jesus already gave you that when He commissioned you in Matthew 28:19–20 and when He rose with all power in His hands, declaring that He had taken the keys from death, hell, and the grave (Revelation 1:18).

Hope begins in brokenness and gives you permission to believe again. Healing takes root in surrender and invites you to be honest again. Wholeness comes as we walk daily with the Breath of God leading us and calls us to live free again.

You don't have to wait until you feel strong to start.

You are not walking alone. God is with you. His breath is in you. And I'm cheering for you, every step of the way.

Take a deep breath. Let Ruach fill the room.

Let's begin.

Sharonda N. Thomas

Part One

Hope: Awakening the Possibility

"Hope is not a feeling. It's your anchor in the storm and your weapon in the war."

" This hope is a strong and trustworthy anchor for our souls. It leads us through the curtain into God's inner sanctuary" Hebrews 6:19 (NLT)

Prayer

Father, thank You for being the anchor of my soul. Even when storms come, You remain steady. Help me to understand the power of hope today. Breathe fresh life into my heart. In Jesus' name, Amen.

Chapter 1

What is Hope?

I didn't just stumble upon hope. I was born into it. I was raised in the pews of Call Community COGIC until the age of ten, where the scent of anointing oil mixed with the echo of hymns in wood-framed walls. My paternal grandmother, who passed when I was six, was the church mother. She was a woman of dignity and discipline who taught us that no act of service was too small when done unto the Lord. She was the mother of eighteen children. She earnestly prayed that her children and grandchildren would be saved, and she was a great example of living a hope-filled life. Her life example and the daughters she raised were my mother's introduction to a relationship with Christ. My mother, Elder Angela Bennett, has been both my pastor and my blueprint. She didn't just preach, she lived the gospel, day by day, moment by moment. When she knelt to pray, heaven responded. When she worshipped, chains broke. She didn't raise me to survive; she raised me to stand. I come from a line of women who carried glory in their bones and fire in their mouths.

I didn't understand it fully then, but seeds were being planted. Seeds of endurance. Seeds of faith. Seeds of hope. The kind of hope that doesn't just sing on Sunday but holds you on Monday when everything is falling apart. The kind of hope that outlives grief, grows through pain, and shows up even in silence. Paul wrote to Timothy in 2 Timothy 1:5, "*I am reminded of your sincere faith, which first lived in your grandmother Lois and in your mother Eunice and, I am persuaded, now lives in you also.*" That scripture isn't just historical, it's personal. It's a mirror to my own story. Like Timothy, I carry a generational mantle of faith. Hope didn't begin with me. It's the inheritance I walk in. It's the thread that ties my story to theirs. Healing often begins when we realize that the pain we endured did not destroy the legacy we carry. We are the prayers of generations past, now living out their faith in real-time, and that is where my hope began.

Hope is your anchor. "*We have this hope as an anchor for the soul, firm and secure*" Hebrews 6:19. Hope tethers your spirit to God's truth when life tries to unravel you. Anchors keep you in place during the storm and connect you to something stronger than yourself. Hope is the anchor that proves his love. Hope is not just a wishful thought or a fragile feeling. It is a living, breathing testament of God's love toward us. In 1 Corinthians 13:13, after describing what love is, what it feels like, and what it looks like, Paul makes a bold statement: "*And now these three remain: faith, hope, and love. But the greatest of these is love.*" Many have preached and taught about the supremacy of love, but few slow down to explore the placement of hope within this divine triad.

It is true, you cannot have one without the other. They work hand in hand, together, to build a better you. Hope sits right in the middle. It is not a lesser virtue but the quiet strength between what we believe (faith) and what we live out (love). Hope is proof that God's love is not just something He showed us at the cross; it's something He continues to show us in the present and promises to fulfill in the future. Evidence of a love that has not let go is to still have hope in the middle of loss, pain, delay, or disappointment. It is God's love that whispers to us, "Keep going." It is His love that keeps the heart soft and the eyes lifted. When everything around you suggests giving up, it is love that fuels hope, and hope that proves love is still alive in you. When anxiety and fear attempt to stop you from moving forward, it is God's love and the hope that tells you there is more.

Hope is the first glimpse of light in the darkness. God calls us to hope even in brokenness. Before healing can ever begin, there must be hope. Hope is the whisper that says, "You are not stuck here forever." It is the first flicker of light in a soul that has grown weary from wounds. Many people believe they must wait until they "feel better" to find hope. But in God's Kingdom, hope meets you in your brokenness, not after it. Without hope, we stay paralyzed. Hope is the courage to believe that healing is not only possible but promised. Faith needs hope to move forward, and love fuels both. Hope partners with faith to declare: "I may be broken right now, but God is not finished with me yet." You do not need to be healed to have hope. You need hope to be healed. Healing is a journey. Wholeness is the destination. Hope is the spark that ignites the first step forward, and love is the hand that holds you through the entire way.

In Hebrew, the word for hope is "Tikvah," meaning expectation or cord. It paints a picture of being tied to God's promises like a lifeline, even when life feels like it's unraveling. Tikvah is not passive, but it's confident waiting with expectation that something good will come to pass. *"For I know the plans I have for you," declares the Lord, "plans to prosper you and not to harm you, plans to give you a future and a hope (tikvah)"* Jeremiah 29:11. In this verse, God isn't just offering wishful thinking, but a firm expectation rooted in His unchanging nature. Hope is not just a feeling; it's a spiritual tether to God's promises that holds you steady when everything else is uncertain. In the Greek of the New Testament, hope is the word "Elpis", a joyful and confident expectation that God will fulfill what He has spoken. *"May the God of hope (Elpis) fill you with all joy and peace as you trust in him..."* Romans 15:13

(NIV) Elpis is a confident assurance deeply rooted in the joyful expectation that God will do what He said, because Christ has already secured it through His life, death, and resurrection.

Build your Hope

Throughout Scripture, we witness how hope is not a passive posture but an active expression of trust in the love of God. Hope is not wishful thinking, but it is the living proof that God's love is still working, even when the evidence seems scarce.

I'm reminded of Abraham's hope when it looked impossible. Romans 4:18 says, *"Against all hope, Abraham in hope believed..."* God had promised him descendants as numerous as the stars, yet he and Sarah was old, and her womb was barren. The facts were discouraging, and Sarah even laughed at the thought of it being possible, but hope kept Abraham aligned with God's promise. Abraham's hope was not rooted in his ability to produce; it was anchored in God's faithfulness to fulfill. He submitted and surrendered to the sovereignty of God, no matter what it looked like, no matter the mess he made, the barrenness of his wife's womb, or her unbelief.

Hannah hoped amid rejection. She cried out to the Lord year after year for a child, mocked by Peninnah and misunderstood even by Eli the priest. Yet she kept coming back to the temple, pouring out her soul. Her hope didn't rest on human affirmation, but on the loving nature of a God who hears.

He did hear, and Samuel was born from a womb filled with faith and a heart filled with hope. Hope was her evidence that God's love was still working on her behalf, even when others couldn't see it.

I have experienced this type of love through the hope of God's promises. Due to illness, I was told I may not be able to have children. Imagine my joy when I learned I was pregnant with my first child. I carried that precious sweet little girl in my womb for twenty weeks before experiencing severe cramping. I can remember the moment I was told I would have to endure labor until her birth, and that there was a high probability of loss due to Gabrielle not having any lung development. I was heartbroken. Then I got pregnant again, with Nicholas, and I carried him for sixteen weeks before I devastatingly went into labor once again. After his loss, I thought, I'm not meant to carry a baby or be a mother; something is wrong with me. I can remember longing to leave this world and be in Heaven with my babies.

Sitting on the side of the bed, God's love interrupted my hopeless heart with a promise that I would carry children, and I would be a mother. Today, I have three beautiful boys that God allowed me to carry to full term and be their mother. Gerald, my husband of twenty-one years, and I were grateful and blessed to have the first two boys. We decided two were enough upon the doctor's recommendation and because of the pain of carrying them. So, I got a tubal ligation, a surgical procedure meant to sterilize females from being able to get pregnant. Exactly five years later, I found out I was pregnant again, and the pregnancy was viable. God blessed us over and beyond what we could have ever hoped for. All three of our boys are my Samuel's born from a womb filled with faith and a heart of hope!

Then there is David, who was anointed king and sent back into his father's field to tend the sheep. After serving, honoring, and loving his leader, Saul, David spent years running from him, hiding in caves, wrestling with discouragement and betrayal. Yet he wrote in Psalm 42:11, *"Why, my soul, are you downcast? ... Put your hope in God, for I will yet praise Him, my Savior and my God."* Hope didn't mean he wasn't hurting; it meant he knew God loved him enough not to leave him in the cave. That hope carried David through dark seasons until the promise was fulfilled.

Consider the woman with the issue of blood for twelve long years. Twelve years of bleeding. Twelve years of being labeled "unclean." Twelve years of disappointment. But when she heard about Jesus, her hope stirred again. She didn't just believe in a miracle; she believed in His heart. The Heart of God - living, breathing, walking on earth. The heart that would never leave her the way she was. Her heart was filled with hope. Hope that He would turn, see her, and that love would make room for her. Her hope reached out, and love stopped in its tracks. Her hope flung her out into the open world that shunned her and her faith that said, *"for she said to herself, 'If I only touch his garment, I will be made well."* Matthew 9:21 ESV.

So, build your hope. Lay the foundation with truth. Let the walls rise with faith. Let the roof be grace, and the windows mercy, and through it all, let love be the builder because hope is not the end of your story. It's the bridge between your brokenness and your breakthrough. What is hope speaking to you today? Build on that.

Don't Let Hope Die in the Middle

There's a place between the promise and the breakthrough. A space many of us never prepare for. It's the middle. The middle is dry and unclear. It's where you're too far from where you started and not yet close enough to where you're going. I remember a vision I had of seeing myself there once. Standing in what looked like a field, all around me was flat, lifeless, covered in dry, grey sand. A house, a barn, and a strange stillness surrounded me. The sun wasn't shining, and the sky was grey. In every direction I looked, I could see storms. In those storms were tornadoes that spun like threats waiting to strike. In this vision, I had three choices: I could run back, but behind me was darker, heavier, hopeless. I could stay there, sit in fear, hide, take cover, and pretend the storms wouldn't reach me. Or I could keep going because even through the shadows, I saw a silver lining up ahead. That moment felt like I was Jonah in the belly of the whale. There was no clear escape. Just surrender... and hope. Hope was the only thing pushing me forward. Hope reminded me: "This middle is not your final destination."

Psalm 23:4 reminds us that God doesn't lead us around the valley; He walks with us through it. Even when the path is shadowed by fear and uncertainty, we cling to the confession: "I *will fear no evil, for You are with me.*" His presence is our peace. His rod and staff don't just guide us, they comfort and protect us every step of the way. Likewise, Jonah's cry from the depths in Jonah 2 echoes this truth: *"From the belly of Sheol I cried, and You heard my voice."* Even in our darkest places, God hears. God stays. God saves.

The middle tests your vision. This place will test everything that you ever thought you knew. It will humble you. The middle challenges your memory of what God said and your faith to not be moved from what you believe. The middle is also where God builds your perseverance, strengthens your faith, and teaches you to walk when you can't see the finish line. Don't let hope die in the middle because when you press forward, you'll realize what looked like dry sand was actually holy ground. The storm couldn't kill you. The whale couldn't hold you. And hope? It never left you. It was carrying you forward the entire time. As Hebrews 10:35-36 reminds us *not throw away your confidence because it will be richly rewarded.*

Hope Is a Weapon

Hope isn't just something we feel. It's something we fight with. Hope is a weapon of spiritual warfare. It silences despair, disarms discouragement, and displaces depression. Hope says: "I still believe God, even here." When the enemy tries to shake your faith, he usually starts with your hope because if he can drain your hope, your faith and prayers weaken too. Hope breaks the cycle. It doesn't always roar. Sometimes, it whispers. But even then, it wages war. Hope is heaven's refusal to agree with hell.

We see this so clearly in the Story of Elijah. He stood in boldness on Mount Carmel, calling down fire from heaven in a dramatic showdown with the prophets of Baal (1 Kings 18). One man, armed only with faith, hope, and the word of the Lord, faced hundreds. Yet hope roared through him that day, and heaven answered. Fire fell, the people repented, and God got the victory. But isn't it something… that the very next chapter, after such a powerful moment, Elijah ran? Fear took hold of his heart because Jezebel threatened his life. Elijah fled into the wilderness, finally collapsing in a cave, overwhelmed and alone. Yet, even there, hope whispered again. God did not meet him in the earthquake, nor did He answer with fire this time. He wasn't in the wind or the chaos; instead, He spoke in a still small voice. Hope doesn't always need a stage. Sometimes it meets you in the cave with a whisper that says, "You're not done. I'm still with you. You're not alone." Hope isn't naive; it's prophetic. Hope says: God still loves me, even here." "This is not the end." "His love isn't finished with me yet." If you still have hope, even a flicker, it's not because you're strong with your own strength. It's because God's love is holding space for your future. Elijah wasn't abandoned. He was being recommissioned, and so are you. Hope may look small, but in the spirit it's deadly to despair. Keep fighting with hope.

Before We Begin: The Weight We Carry

Before you leave this chapter and build your hope, you must be honest about what broke you. You may be tempted to skip ahead to rush toward healing, faith, purpose, and joy. But if you do that without addressing the grief that's still tangled in your soul, it won't last. Unhealed pain doesn't stay buried. It resurfaces in self-doubt, control, anxiety, shutdowns, or cycles that make you ask, "How did I end up here again?" So, pause here. Breathe. And ask yourself:

- What am I still grieving?
- What did I hope would happen, but it didn't?
- What was taken from me? Whether suddenly or slowly?
- Where do I still carry shame for not seeing it sooner or stopping it in time?

- What am I afraid to admit… even to God?

We don't ask these questions to punish ourselves, but we ask them to bring them into the light, where healing lives. Healing is allowing yourself to grieve the what-ifs, to grieve what should have been, and to grieve the version of yourself that believed this wouldn't be your story. Whether you know it or not, you are already grieving; now you need to acknowledge it. That grief is not a betrayal of your faith. It is preparation for real hope. These are the questions that echo in silent tears and sleepless nights. Sometimes we whisper it with blame and other times with bewilderment.

- How did I let it go on for so long?
- How did I silence my voice?
- How did I keep loving what kept wounding me?
- Why didn't I see the signs?
- Why did I believe this was all I deserved?

There may not be a single answer. If I am honest, I haven't found one, but here's what I know: God is not afraid of the questions. He meets us in them, not with condemnation, but with clarity, comfort, and sometimes confrontation that heals. This chapter is not to fix you. It's to invite you to feel before you try to fix. You must be willing to be honest and surrender to

God in all His sovereignty. When you do, you'll be ready for what comes next.

Reflection

What promise from God can you anchor your soul to today, even if you can't see it yet?

- What intentional steps can you take this week to build or rebuild your hope in God's faithfulness?
- In what area of your life do you need to stop retreating and start fighting back with hope?
- What burden have you been silently carrying that you need to lay down so hope can take root?

Prophetic Declaration

My best days are not behind me; they are still ahead. There is still more that God has assigned for me to do. My hope is alive and sustained by the promises of God. I am moving from despair into divine hope. I choose to dwell in hope, to stand firm in it, and to speak from it. I am anchored in the unshakable hope found in Christ Jesus. Hope is my position, my posture, and my portion. He who promised is faithful (Hebrews 10:23), and He is able to do exceedingly, abundantly above all that I could ever ask or think, according to His power that is at work within me (Ephesians 3:20).

Let this declaration be more than words; it be a banner over your life today. Amen.

Chapter 2

Recognizing Seeds of Hope

God doesn't always thunder His presence from the heavens. Sometimes, He doesn't split the sky open or part the sea. Sometimes, He comes quietly and gently like a whisper that brushes your soul and causes you to lean in just a little closer.

In 1 Kings 19, Elijah is drained. He is filled with anxiety, fear, suicidal thoughts, and extremely overwhelmed with the threats. He has been convinced that he is the only prophet of the Lord c that is left. He's been in what I like to call the *Valley of the Great Showdown*. In this showdown, he's just seen God send fire from heaven, defeat false prophets, and demonstrate His power in a bold and visible way. But not long after that,

Elijah receives threats that he knows can really happen from Jezebel. He now finds himself running for forty days to Mount Sinani and is hiding in a cave, afraid and exhausted, asking God to take his life. What Elijah needed in that moment wasn't more fire. He didn't need another display of power. He needed the presence of God in a way that provided peace to the mental warfare. That's when God whispered.

Sometimes, hope shows up like that. In a whisper. It doesn't come roaring through your storm or shaking your foundation or setting things on fire. Although, hope can come in loud and boisterous. Sometimes it shows up in a soft word during prayer. In a stranger's smile when you needed encouragement. It's lyrics in a song. In a random Scripture that just so happens to be the exact thing your soul needed that day.

You might think, "That's too small to be God." But the whisper is how God speaks when He's close. You don't have to shout when He's nearby. God whispers because He's not distant, Quite the opposite, He's right there, breathing hope into the places where you've gone quiet from pain or fear. He won't allow fear to run you in a cave or silence you, he simply comforts you sends you peace and calmest way possible.

I know this whisper well. I've heard it in caves, emotional and spiritual. I've stood on stages leading worship and preaching the gospel in the boldness of fire, only to flee into hiding when fear of failure crept in. There were seasons when I longed for the voice and covering of a father but instead found myself wrapped in the attention and approval of leaders. At some point, I stopped just listening to their advice and I gave them authority in places only God should have ruled. I ultimately put my trust in leaders instead of God. Somewhere along the way, I had made them an idol, giving them the seat on the throne of my heart that only God deserved. They sat on that throne, shaping my decisions, my identity, and even how I saw the Lord. But idols always crumble under the weight of misplaced worship. When the foundation of that throne faltered, I was left not just with disappointment, but with the realization that I had to repent for giving man what only belongs to God. That was the beginning of true healing. When I dethroned people and re-enthroned Christ as the only voice, authority, and source of my hope.

"Then he said, "Son of man, dig into the wall." So, I dug into the wall and found a hidden doorway. "Go in," he said, "and see the wicked and detestable sins they are committing in there!" So, I went in and saw the walls covered with engravings of all kinds of crawling animals and detestable creatures. I also saw the various idols worshiped by the people of Israel. Seventy leaders of Israel were standing there with Jaazaniah son of Shaphan in the center. Each of them held an incense burner, from which a cloud of incense rose above their heads. Then the Lord said to me, "Son of man, have you seen what the leaders of Israel are doing with their idols in dark rooms? They are saying, 'The Lord doesn't see us; he has deserted our land!'"

Then the Lord added, "Come, and I will show you even more detestable sins than these!" Ezekiel 8:8–13

Ezekiel 8:8–13 came alive to me. Like the prophet, God asked me to dig into the walls I had built to expose the hidden places of compromise and deception. He showed me that even leaders can operate in darkness while still holding incense. That sobering truth didn't make me bitter. It made me bold. Bold enough to talk to someone: a counselor, a friend, a small group, my spouse. I learned that if I "Confess your sins to each other and pray for each other so that you may be healed. The earnest prayer of a righteous person has great power and produces wonderful results." (James 5:16 NLT)

Here's the mystery of it all: the place of my deepest wound became the wellspring of my greatest worship. What hurt me didn't get the final word. Hope did. The manipulation didn't steal my praise. The silence didn't rob me of God's sound. Instead, it made me more sensitive to His voice and more rooted in His truth. I learned to separate the vessel from the voice. I learned that the failure of man does not cancel the faithfulness of God. That's when I saw the ground being cleared. That's when I heard the plow break the surface. That's when I realized: this pain isn't just punishment. It's preparation. Look for the seeds: small, large, whispers or shouts. Hope is there.

The Power of Small Beginnings

Before you plant, you must clear the ground. No farmer starts a garden by throwing seeds on top of weeds. The first step is clearing the land. The plow breaks up the hardened ground. The farmer exposes what lies just beyond the grass. He pulls up roots of weeds that could choke out his seeds. He removes rocks, burns away thorns, and flattens the uneven places. It's not pretty work. It's gritty, sweaty, back-breaking work.

Then there comes a moment when the ground is cleared, and the seeds are planted but nothing is growing. The sun rises and rain comes. You pray. You worship. You believe. And still... the soil stays quiet. You start looking for any sign. Shouldn't something be sprouting by now? Did I plant it right? Was the seed bad? Did I miss my season? The silence between sowing and sprouting can feel like failure. But this is tension of faith. Every farmer knows: the seed dies before it lives. It goes into hiding dark place before it breaks through.

Growth is always silent before it becomes seen. So, what do you do when there's no visible progress? You pray, stay steady, expose to the sun(son) light, water, worship and wait. You stand assured that the ground is now prepared correctly and there will be fruit.

That is what the beginning of healing feels like too. You don't start with fruit. You start with a mess, with a dirty mess that is full of weeds, rocks and uneven places. You know those painful memories, the gut-wrenching regret, the many unanswered questions, and emotional overgrowth. Things that didn't just appear overnight they built up over time. The erection of the man on the throne of your heart did not happen overnight. It happened over time. And God, in His mercy, puts a plow to your soul and says: "Let Me make this ground ready again." Clearing the ground doesn't always look like progress. But it is. Even when it doesn't look like anything is happening, something is happening deep beneath the surface. Hope is being formed in the soil of surrender.

Some of the most powerful beginnings don't start with boldness. They start with tears. They start with saying, "I thought it would look different by now." They begin when you sit in the wreckage of what didn't grow and still dare to pick up the shovel. Here, you grieve the what-ifs, the should-haves, and the why-didn'ts. You walk through the "how did I get here?" "How did I let this happens?" And still… you choose to plant something new.

But you don't stay there. You pick up the seed of hope and you plant again because hope is not built on pretending. It's built on planting. It's not the absence of disappointment; it's the decision to believe anyway. It's not ignoring your past; it's choosing not to let it have the final say. Hope is holy defiance. It says: "Even after all that, I still believe God will bring a harvest."

Faith: Walking Without Seeing

Faith is the decision to put a seed in the ground when all you see is dirt. It's trusting that the soil will do what it was created to do, even when it looks like nothing is happening. It's having enough spiritual vision to believe that something is becoming, even when your natural eyes can't yet see it. Faith is the yes you give before you understand the full assignment. It is showing up for what God said even when your feelings don't align, your resources don't measure up, and your surroundings seem stuck. Just like a gardener bends down in faith, placing a tiny seed into broken ground, we, too, must lower ourselves in humility and obedience, believing that the same God who gives seed to the sower will bring increase in due time.

No one embodies this kind of gritty, surrendering faith more beautifully than Ruth. Ruth's story doesn't begin with breakthrough; it begins with devastation. She loses her husband, her future, her security, and everything familiar to her in Moab. Naomi, her mother-in-law, becomes bitter and hopeless, telling Ruth and Orpah to return to their people. Orpah leaves. But Ruth, somehow, sees something worth following, not in Naomi's circumstances, but in her God. Ruth makes a choice that faith often demands: to follow not because of proof, but because of presence.

"Where you go, I will go. Where you stay, I will stay. Your people will be my people and your God my God" (Ruth 1:16). With no promise in hand and no guarantee of provision, Ruth clings to Naomi and walks into a foreign land with nothing but a broken heart and a made-up mind.

I know that feeling. I've lived it. After leaving the ministry I had been a part of for twenty years. The place where I had served, grown, and poured out so much of my life, I found myself in unfamiliar territory. I was walking away from the familiar, the routine, the titles, and the comfort. While I knew God was leading me forward, everything in my flesh screamed uncertainty. I felt like I had stepped into a foreign land with nothing but a broken heart and a made-up mind. Every decision felt heavy and unsure. But the guidance of God's voice was clear: Don't turn back. Don't go back to what I've delivered you from.

I picked up a phrase during that season that still defines how I walk with God today: "I'm just out here trusting God." That's it. That's the posture. That's the declaration. It means I heard His voice, I said yes, and I kept walking without a map, without certainty, without knowing what I would walk up on or what would meet me along the way. Just faith, obedience and God.

Imagine the weight of that journey walking away from her homeland, her community, her memories, her comfort. Ruth carried pain in one hand and hope in the other. That's what faith looks like when you're healing. It's not sanitized. It's not easy. It's not always confident. Sometimes faith is tired steps in the direction of God while your heart still aches from what you lost. But every step Ruth took was sowing something into the soil of her future and even though she couldn't see it, God was already orchestrating her redemption. When Ruth arrived in Bethlehem, she didn't sit and wait for favor; she got to work. She gleaned in the fields, picking up scraps behind the harvesters.

That's how faith works. You show up to the hard place. You glean. You bend low again and again, trusting that each day you're gathering just enough grace to get through. What Ruth didn't know was that the field she found herself in belonged to Boaz, her kinsman-redeemer. Her faith led her to the very place her redemption had already been planted because God is a Master Gardener. He plans your harvest before you even know to sow the seed.

And your tears? They are not signs of weakness; they are part of the process. Your tears are watering the ground. They are saturating the roots of your obedience. Ruth wept, surely, for what she lost. But her tears didn't hinder her future; they hydrated it. *"Weeping may endure for a night, but joy comes in the morning."* Psalm 30:5. Joy doesn't erase what you've been through, but it proves that you didn't die there. Faith doesn't eliminate the wilderness; it teaches you how to walk through it. Faith doesn't ignore the pain; it just refuses to let pain have the final word. Ruth never said, "I'm okay." She just said, "I'm going." That's faith. You don't have to be fearless; you just have to be willing.

Faith says, "I don't see the harvest yet, but I'm still planting." Faith says, "I don't know how God will do it, but I believe He will." Faith says, "Even if this looks like a grave, I will treat it like a garden."

Your steps of obedience are not being wasted. Your pain is not wasted. The seed of faith you're sowing now is falling into the very ground God will use to grow something beautiful. You are walking into fields you didn't plant because God has already made provision for your faith.

So, pick up your shovel. Plant again. Walk forward like Ruth, with your grief in your heart and your trust in God's hands. The field you're stepping into has already been chosen and the harvest is on the way.

Nurturing the Seed

Not every heart is ready for a harvest. That's not to shame anyone it's simply the truth Jesus reveals in Luke 8:15. In the parable of the Sower, we learn that the seed is always good. It's the soil that determines the outcome. Jesus says, *"But the seed on good soil stands for those with a noble and good heart, who hear the word, retain it, and by persevering produce a crop."* That one verse is full of revelation: good soil hears the Word, holds onto it, and doesn't give up when growth feels slow.

We all want the fruit, but we don't always want the breaking. Yet before soil can receive a seed, it must be broken and disturbed. That's exactly what prayer does in the life of the believer. Prayer plows through the hardness in our hearts. The parts trampled by disappointment, packed down by pain, or overrun with self-protection. Prayer isn't always eloquent; sometimes it sounds like a sigh, a moan or groan, a whispered, "God, help me", or a gut-wrenching weep. Those cries are prayers. They are evidence that your soil is being turned and that your heart, though wounded, is still reaching for Him.

Once the ground is broken, it needs to be watered. That's what the Word of God does. It soaks into the dry places and awakens the hidden potential beneath the surface. It reminds your soul what is true when everything around you feels unsure. The Word anchors you when your emotions want to drift. It gives substance to your hope. Not because it erases reality, but because it declares a greater reality. One where God finishes what He starts. One where those who sow in tears will reap in joy. One where a mustard seed of faith can still move mountains.

Even with soft soil and fresh water, growth doesn't happen overnight. Luke 8:15 says that, *"good soil produces a crop through perseverance."* That means sticking with the process when you're tempted to quit and returning to the same field day after day even when nothing looks different. Perseverance is holy repetition. It's praying, believing and trusting again and again. It's letting hope take root in you, even when you feel tired or unsure because what's planted in faith doesn't just survive but thrives under pressure.

Even the healthiest garden needs the right environment. Meaning you need voices around you who speak life, who protect what's growing, and who remind you of what God said when your own memory starts to fade. Community doesn't make your seed grow but it can help keep the weeds from choking it out. It can help you endure the wait between sowing and reaping and remind you, "Don't give up. The harvest is coming."

So, ask the Lord to make your heart good soil. Not just soft, but strong. Not just ready but rooted. Not just nurturing but healthy. Let Him break what needs to be broken. Let Him water what's been dry. Let Him guard what you've planted and stretch your capacity to persevere. Because this is the promise: if you hold on, if you keep tending your garden with faith and patience, you will produce a harvest. *"Let us not become weary in doing good, for at the proper time we will reap a harvest if we do not give up."* Galatians 6:9 (NIV)

Recognizing the Signs of Growth

Growth rarely announces itself with fanfare. It doesn't shout or demand attention. Most of the time, it happens quietly, hidden beneath the surface, deep in the places no one else can see. That's why so many people miss the signs of breakthrough. They expect fireworks when the first sign of a harvest might look like a tiny green shoot pushing through cracked, dry soil. Galatians 6:9 is not just a verse; it's a rhythm. It teaches us that reaping doesn't follow immediately after sowing. There's a space between the work and the reward. A stretch of time where the only evidence you have is that you haven't given up. That's where most of the growth happens, and that's where hope is often tested.

You might be looking around right now wondering, "Where's the fruit? Where's the fulfillment? Where's the evidence that what I've been doing is working?" But the Word says there will be a harvest if you don't faint, if you don't quit, if you keep going. Hope doesn't just believe for the destination it learns to recognize the small signs along the way.

Maybe the sign of growth in this season isn't a major breakthrough, but a shift in how you respond. In the moments that happen that you later recognize. The moments you didn't react in anger, you prayed instead of panicked, you slept through the night for the first time in months, you set a boundary, or you laughed again. These may seem small, but spiritually, they are massive indicators that healing and hope is rising, that the seed is germination and that something is growing.

Growth isn't just about results it's about resilience. Are you getting stronger in the waiting? Are you more anchored than you used to be? Are you still saying yes to God, even though you haven't seen the full picture yet? That is growth. That is evidence that your heart is good soil, and the seed is doing its job even if the harvest hasn't shown itself in full.

Yes, growth can be exhausting. There are days when you'll feel like nothing's changing. When you've prayed the same prayers, shown up the same way, done the right thing and still feel like you're walking in circles. But the Word reminds us: don't grow weary. Don't let weariness become your lens. Don't confuse slow growth with no growth. Heaven sees what's happening, and the harvest is scheduled for an appointed time not your time, but the right time. The garden of your life may not be bursting with fruit just yet, but if you look closely, something is happening. That tenderness you feel again? That hunger for the Word? That willingness to forgive or believe again? Those are your green shoots. Those are signs that you're not stuck, you're growing. So, take heart, stay faithful, and keep tending your field even when it feels quiet and looks empty, because in God's perfect timing, the harvest always comes. When it does, it will be more than worth the wait.

Reflection

- What is one area of your life where God is inviting you to start again, even if it looks small or uncertain?

- What step of obedience is God asking you to take, even though you can't yet see the outcome?

- How are you actively tending to the promises God has planted in your heart?

- What is God revealing to you about the condition of your heart, and how is He preparing it for growth?

- What small but meaningful signs of spiritual growth or healing have you seen in yourself recently?

Prophetic Declaration of Hope

I will not confuse quiet seasons with barren ones. Silence does not mean stagnation. I trust the Lord of the harvest, even in the waiting. I am content to be still while God cultivates greatness within me. In His perfect timing, the harvest will come, and it will be abundant, purposeful, and beautiful. I believe that what God produces in my life will far exceed anything I could produce in my strength. I wait with hope, knowing that His timing is always right and His work in me is never wasted. Amen.

Chapter 3

When Hope Hurts

Before we go any further in this journey, let's establish something necessary: faith does not cancel out emotion. God never shows us that we are not going to experience pain, grief, or despair. He does show us in his word how not to lose hope amid the pain. Two things can be true at the same time. You can believe in God and still feel pain. You can trust His promises, but there are still days when the tears don't stop. You can be full of the Spirit and still wrestle with sorrow, grief, confusion, or disappointment. It is in the crushing, painful moments that hope is there, shining the light in the darkness. If you've ever been made to feel like crying meant you didn't believe or that acknowledging your heartbreak somehow made you less faithful, hear this clearly: that is not the truth of Scripture, nor the heart of God. Faith is not the absence of feeling. Faith is the act of holding God's hand while you feel.

We see this truth lived out in David, the man after God's own heart. Read through the Psalms and you'll find a man who poured out raw emotion in the presence of God, grief, rage, fear, shame, even despair. He wrote things like, "How long, O Lord? Will you forget me forever?" (Psalm 13:1) and "Why are you so far from saving me, so far from my cries of anguish?" (Psalm 22:1). And yet, God never rebuked David for his honesty. He welcomed it. David wasn't less faithful because he hurt; he was deeply faithful because he brought his hurt to God, instead of hiding it. Then there's Hannah. She was barren, misunderstood, and aching with the unmet desire to be a mother. In 1 Samuel 1:10, it says she prayed in "bitterness of soul and wept much." Her pain was not polite, nor was it filtered. She wept with her whole body. So much so, the priest thought she was drunk. But God accepted her, met her, honored her, and opened her womb.

These stories remind us that God doesn't require you to numb your feelings in order to prove your faith. He wants all of it. The trembling hands, the broken voice, the whispered, "God, I don't understand." That's not weakness. That's relationship. So, if you're carrying sadness or confusion into this book, you're not doing it wrong. You're doing it REAL. You're doing it like

David. like Hannah and like Jesus in the garden. You don't need to pretend you're okay to qualify for healing. You don't need to smile through your sorrow to earn God's attention. Bring your full self here. Let the tears come if they need to. Let the questions rise if they must. Let your heart break open in His presence because that's the kind of soil where true hope begins to grow.

The Weight of Hoping While Bleeding

Hope is beautiful, but it isn't always light. Sometimes it's heavy. Sometimes it's bloody. Sometimes it's carrying a promise with one hand and wiping away tears with the other. Hope doesn't always feel like sunlight and breakthrough. Sometimes it feels like labor: groaning, pressing, breaking. The passage from Luke 8:43-48 gives us a holy picture of this kind of hope. It says:

A woman in the crowd had suffered for twelve years with constant bleeding, and she could find no cure. Coming up behind Jesus, she touched the fringe of his robe. Immediately, the bleeding stopped. "Who touched me?" Jesus asked. Everyone denied it, and Peter said, "Master, this whole crowd is pressing up against you." But Jesus said, "Someone deliberately touched me, for I felt healing power go out from me." When the woman realized that she could not stay hidden, she began to tremble and fell to her knees in front of him. The whole crowd heard her explain why she had touched him and that she had been immediately healed. "Daughter," he said to her, "your faith has made you well. Go in peace." (Luke 8:43-48, NLT)

She had been bleeding for twelve years. Physically suffering, emotionally exhausted, spiritually isolated. She was ceremonially unclean, which meant she lived in rejection and shame, shut out from worship, touch, and connection. Yet, hope made her reach. Her act of faith wasn't loud. It wasn't announced. It was a crawl. A trembling hand reached for the edge of a garment, and it was enough. This is precisely what it means to carry hope while bleeding. Her hope didn't wait until the bleeding stopped. It didn't wait for her strength to return. It reached through the crowd, through fear, through disappointment, through years of silence and shame. She didn't wait to be whole to hope; she hoped as she reached. She believed as she wept. She trusted as she trembled, and heaven responded.

I've bled while hoping. I've sat in hospital rooms, hearing words that tried to drain the faith right out of me. I've birthed children I never got to raise. I've sat on the edge of my bed and begged God to take me home. Yet, in those moments, I still believed; barely, weakly, quietly. But I did. That's the weight of hope. It's not loud. It's not always bold. Sometimes, it's the whisper of, "I'm just out here trusting God," while your body is breaking, and your heart is bruised. Hope in this place is holy. It's not cheap or shallow. It's drenched in tears, pain, and worship that doesn't need a song. It's the offering of a heart that says, "Even if I bleed again tomorrow, I still believe today."

God wants you to know: the bleeding is not for your shame but for His Glory. The brokenness is not your disqualification. It's your altar. It's the place where His glory meets your grief. He's not asking you to hide it. He's asking you to bring it. Because when you crawl forward in faith, even through the blood, Heaven responds. His power is drawn to your weakness, and His glory is revealed through your pressing. Hope is not the absence of pain; it is the refusal to let pain speak the final word. Like the woman who bled for twelve years, many of us know what it is to carry a silent suffering that no one sees. But the hem of His garment is still enough. The reach still matters, and your faith, no matter how small, still moves Him.

Jesus knew what it was to hurt, what it was to hope, and what it meant to surrender. Hope doesn't always feel strong. Sometimes it feels heavy. Even Jesus experienced the pain of hope. In the Garden of Gethsemane, under such emotional stress, He sweated drops of blood, a rare condition called *hematidrosis*. This happens under extreme agony, as blood vessels burst around sweat glands. Under the weight of what was to come, He didn't hide His agony. He brought it into the presence of the Father. His heart was breaking under the weight of what He was about to endure. And yet He prayed: *"Father, if it be possible, let this cup pass from Me... nevertheless, not My will, but Yours be done."* (Luke 22:42)

This moment is not weakness; it's worship. It's not doubt, it's devotion. Jesus wasn't asking to escape purpose; He was simply bringing His full humanity into His divine assignment. He showed us that real surrender happens in the same breath as real pain. Jesus shows us that surrender is not weakness, but it's the beginning of strength. It's where hope gets purified and where heaven aligns with earth. The garden wasn't where Jesus failed; it was where He was fortified. *"Now my soul is troubled, and what shall I say? 'Father, save me from this hour'? No, it was for this very reason I came to this hour."*

Hope can hurt. Not because it's false, but because it asks us to lay down our plans. It asks us to bury our version of the outcome. It requires the death of what we thought life would look like. Hope says, "I trust You, God, even if this doesn't unfold like I imagined." It surrenders the timing. The method. The outcome. It lets go of the fantasy and embraces the faith.

In that garden, Jesus wasn't just praying for Himself; He was modeling what it looks like to hope with holy tension. To say, "I believe in resurrection, but I'm not numb to the cross." To say, "I know this ends in glory, but I still feel the weight of the grief. Sometimes hope asks you to carry the cross before you ever see the crown. Sometimes it takes you through Gethsemane before it leads you to victory. But here's the truth: the garden was not a place of abandonment; it was a place of alignment.

Jesus didn't leave that place defeated. He left strengthened. Resolved. Still hurting, but no longer alone in the hurting. If you're hoping and hurting at the same time, you're not failing; you're following Him. If you've found yourself praying, "God, if it's possible, take this from me," but you're still waking up and saying, "Yet not my will, but Yours," you're in good company. You are walking the same road the Savior walked. And just like Him, you will rise. It's like a seed being buried. *"Unless a kernel of wheat falls to the ground and dies, it remains only a single seed. But if it dies, it produces seeds."* (John 12:24 NLT) Sometimes what we grieve most is not what was but what we imagined it could have been. That's real pain. But it's not without purpose. Hope hurts because it's holy. Jesus shows us: it's possible to hurt and still be held. Hope hurts… but it holds you anyway.

When the Dream Dies

There is a heartbreak few are willing to talk about in church. The heartbreak of doing everything "right" and still not getting the result you prayed for. This is the ache of a dream delayed, of expectations unmet, of promises that felt so close they had a pulse… only to slip away in silence. It's the kind of pain that leaves you asking hard questions: "What else was I supposed to do?" "Wasn't I faithful?" "Did I not believe hard enough?" "Where was God when it was falling apart?" This is where hope gets quiet. Not gone but quiet. It's what Proverbs calls "heart-sick hope." The kind that no longer stands tall, but slumps over. The kind that no longer sings, but sighs. The kind that no longer roars, but whispers through tears, "God, where were You?"

Sometimes what we grieve most is not what was, but what we imagined it could have been. It's not always the reality we bury but the hope we built around it. We grieve the wedding we never had, the child we never held, the ministry we thought would thrive, the business we poured everything into, the relationship we believed would heal, the apology we never received, and the version of ourselves we thought would have emerged by now. We grieve the story we wrote in our minds. The one we prayed for, planned for, and pictured unfolding a certain way. And when that imagined future dies, it can feel harder to mourn than the tangible losses. Because you can't bury what was never born.

That's exactly what Mary and Martha asked in John 11. Their brother Lazarus was dying, and they had sent word to Jesus in time. They didn't doubt His power. They didn't question His love. In fact, the Bible tells us, *"Jesus loved Martha, Mary, and Lazarus..."* (John 11:5 NLT). But when Jesus finally showed up, Lazarus was dead, wrapped, and gone. His sisters were wrecked with grief when they both said the same thing: *"Lord, if you had been here, my brother would not have died."* Those are not words of unbelief. Those are words of a heart in mourning. Words of people who believed, who hoped, who expected, and who still had to bury the dream anyway. But Jesus didn't rebuke them. He didn't say, "You should have had more faith." He didn't correct their theology. He wept with them. Before He resurrected the dead, He stood in the pain of what was lost.

But what about when the dream didn't just die? What about when trauma never allowed it to live? When pain hasn't just delayed the dream but robbed you of the ability to even see one. Trauma doesn't just break your heart; it blinds your vision. It convinces you to settle. It strips the imagination of what could be and cages you in what already is. There was a time in my life when I didn't believe I could be more than someone's secretary. Not because I wasn't gifted or I lacked purpose, but because I was filled with trauma and I was spiritually stunted. Trauma told me I was only what I had survived and that this was as good as it gets. But God… God had more! Little by little, He began to breathe on the dust. He began to show me that even what I forgot, He remembered. Even what I buried in survival, He was ready to resurrect in freedom.

One Saturday morning, during worship and prayer, the Lord stopped me mid-prayer with a truth I didn't expect. I had been operating out of fear. I thought I was protecting my family, covering them, discerning what was best, but really, I was leading from trauma. I was making decisions based on wounds instead of wisdom. I thought I knew best, but in that moment, God whispered something that wrecked me: "You've been in the way of what I want to do." And it cut deep.

I immediately dropped to my knees, weeping and repented. I felt the weight of regret not just for myself, but for how my pain had blocked the dreams and momentum of my household. I felt horrible. But just as quickly, Jesus met me in that pain and with a voice as gentle as a breeze, He whispered again: "I am the Redeemer of time."

That's what delayed hope dares to believe, not just that dreams can rise again, but that even forgotten ones can be restored. That even if you didn't see it before, even if trauma ran the show for far too long, God is big enough to replant the vision and restore the years the locusts ate. If you feel like you missed it, if trauma took it, if shame silenced it, if toxic leaders distorted it, don't worry. Jesus still stands at every tomb, redeems the time, and still calls out what looks dead. He doesn't just raise dreams. He revives dreamers. He is the Resurrection, and when He speaks, even delayed dreams must rise.

Even if hope has grown cold, it can live again. God is the Resurrection and the Life, not just for bodies, but for dreams, for hearts, and futures (John 11:25 NIV). He is the God who restores years, reignites purpose, and resurrects vision. He does not mock your hope, but He honors it. Even the hope you're scared to touch again, He holds it gently.

Stir up your hope again. Stir it through Scripture. Stir it through worship. Stir it through gratitude. Stir it by remembering past victories because if He did it before, He is faithful to do it again. Don't let disappointment disciple you. Let hope lead you.

Your healing requires hope and your hope is never wasted when it's placed in God. *"And this hope will not lead to disappointment. For we know how dearly God loves us..."* (Romans 5:5, NLT)

Let this be your reminder: the dream is not dead; it's just waiting on resurrection.

Reflection and Activation

- When have you felt pressure to hide your pain in order to appear "faithful"? How does knowing David, Hannah, and even Jesus wept reshape your understanding of faith and emotion?
- Can you recall a time when you were "bleeding while hoping"—trusting God in a season of deep pain or loss? What sustained you during that time?
- In what ways have delayed dreams or unfulfilled prayers caused you to question God's presence? How does Jesus' weeping with Mary and Martha speak to your current grief?
- What dreams, visions, or desires have you buried because of trauma, fear, or disappointment? Are there any the Lord is gently asking you to uncover and surrender back to Him?

- How do you respond to the idea that you might have led from trauma instead of healed trust? What would it look like for Jesus to redeem the time and restore the dreams in your life?

Prophetic Declaration

I may be bleeding, but I'm still believing. I may be grieving, but I'm still reaching. I declare that my pain is the end of the story; it is the ground where resurrection begins. I will no longer hide behind strength that was never mine to carry. I bring my whole heart to the Healer, and I trust Him with every broken piece. Though I've buried some dreams, I hear the voice of the Resurrection calling them by name. I decree that every delayed promise is being restored, and the years that were lost to fear and trauma are being redeemed by the Lord. I am not behind. I am not disqualified. I am not forgotten. My hope is not in outcomes. It is in the One who holds time, breathes life, and always keeps His Word. I am held, healed, and rising again. In Jesus' name. Amen

Part Two: Healing
Embracing the Process

Healing is messy and holy. It's God gently repairing what was broken, layer by layer.

"The Spirit of the Lord is upon me, for he has anointed me to bring Good News to the poor. He has sent me to proclaim that captives will be released, that the blind will see, that the oppressed will be set free," Luke 4:18 (NLT)

Prayer:

Jesus, you were anointed to heal the brokenhearted—and today, I bring You mine. I lay before You the pain I've tried to hide, the wounds I've tried to manage, and the pieces I've grown weary of carrying. I trust that Your Spirit is still moving, still binding, still setting the oppressed free. Lord, teach me to embrace the process—not rush it. Help me yield to Your hands as You gently heal what I cannot fix on my own. Be my restorer in the places where I feel undone. Bind every wound with Your mercy and restore every part of me with Your truth. I believe You are faithful to finish what You started. In Jesus' name, Amen.

Chapter 4

The Invitation to Heal

There is a moment in every person's life when pain breaks in uninvited. It doesn't knock, wait, or ask permission. It crashes into your chest and steals the air from your lungs. In those moments when your soul is still trembling, and the tears haven't even had time to dry, God extends the invitation. Not when you have it figured out, not when you've made peace with it or after you've journaled it away or found the "lesson" in it. But right there, while your breath is still caught between sobs and your heart doesn't know how to beat normally again. This is when the invitation is most powerful. Because God does not wait for you to tidy up your grief. He shows up in it. Healing is received, not earned. It begins when we stop covering our wounds and let

God in. "Here I am! I stand at the door and knock." – Revelation 3:20 (NLT)

I want to paint a picture so; I am going to share a few stories about my marriage with you. God sent my husband to me; there's no doubt in my mind. He wasn't just an answer to prayer; he was evidence that heaven hears the cries we whisper in pain. He was my invitation to heal through patient love. He has been, for me, a tangible expression of God's love. Not the kind that's flashy or loud, but the kind that folds laundry when I can't gather my thoughts. The kind that says, "Let's order out," when I'm too exhausted to cook, without making me feel like a failure. The kind that believes in my dreams, even when I'm too weary to chase them myself, and then quietly finds the resources to help make them real. He doesn't just love my body or my ambition; he cares for my soul. He prays with me. He shares his vision with me. He leads me spiritually without crushing my spirit. He has protected me and our peace. He's been a present father to our children, showing them what love looks like when it's consistent, not just convenient. He guards our home: physically, emotionally, spiritually. He builds an atmosphere where healing is possible because peace is preserved.

A great example is, I remember during COVID, when fear and anxiety had gripped the entire world. I got sick. Not just a little sick, violently sick. I couldn't keep anything down. I was vomiting all night and well into the next day. I was so weak that all I could do was lie down. At one point, I looked in the mirror and the white of my eye had a patch of red, like blood had filled it. Fear settled in my chest like a brick. I just knew I had COVID. I had seen too many people succumb to it, and the fear of that was paralyzing. But Gerald never left my side. He held me through the night; he prayed over me and recited scripture when I couldn't even form words. Even when he drifted off to sleep, if I moved even slightly, he'd wake up mid-sentence, still praying. Turns out, I hadn't caught COVID. I had simply overdone it by drinking way too much ginger lemon tea, trying to boost my immune system. The vomiting and stress had ruptured a blood vessel in my eye. I was physically fine. He risked his own life just to stay close and to cover me in intercession. That moment assured me: love isn't proven in easy times. It's proven in the fire. He was my shelter in the storm. Just like Jesus, his love didn't demand that I heal before being held. He held me in my healing.

Another example of this love is that there were times in our marriage when I came into a disagreement, like I was ready to throw down. Emotion running high, pain in my tone, ready to fight just to be heard. And what did he do? He'd look at me, smile a little, shake his head, and say something like, "You're so cute." Not to dismiss me, but to disarm the heat with humor and remind me we were still on the same team. Those little interruptions of tension with tenderness taught me a new way to do family. He showed me that every conflict didn't have to be a battlefield. That love could hold space for emotion without creating war. He showed me that home could be soft, even when life is hard. He showed me that conflict isn't abandonment, that disagreements don't equal disconnection. That I could lash out from old wounds and still be loved, not because it was okay, but because I was still becoming. When I saw the way, he looked at me, even in my mess, I caught a glimpse of the way God sees me. Not as broken but as becoming. Not as too much, but made with care.

Healing often looks like a series of holy invitations. God invites us to heal through situations, safe places, safe people, and safe truths. Sometimes it's in the arms of a spouse, over coffee with a friend, or in the quiet of a counselor's office. Sometimes it's in the whisper of the Holy Spirit, reminding you: "You are still mine." If Jesus is standing at the door and knocking, love is often how He gets your attention. As much as Gerald's love has allowed me to heal and has covered me, I now see it for what it truly is, a living, breathing picture of God's love for each of us. The kind of love that doesn't flinch at our wounds and doesn't grow tired when we're at our weakest. The love that holds us even when our knees are trembling from fear, and our minds are spinning with anxiety. Gerald's love for me reflects an even greater love: the love of Christ Jesus for us all. Jesus is the constant/ He is steady and faithful. He doesn't run from our trauma or hide when we fall apart. He doesn't shame us when we're scared, unsure, or battling to hold onto hope. When anxiety is doing its best to replace the grace and mercy that were promised to follow us all the days of our lives, Jesus is still there. He is still knocking, still waiting, and still offering an invitation.

This is not a one-time call. It's a standing invitation. He is always beckoning us to come closer. Not to perform or pretend, but just to come and draw near. *"For your Creator will be your husband; the Lord of Heaven's Armies is His name! He is your Redeemer, the Holy One of Israel, the God of all the earth"* (Isaiah 54:5 NLT). He is your protector, your provider, your place of peace. Earthly love may fail, but His never will. This is the invitation of healing: not to try harder, but to come home. To collapse into His arms if we must. *"Come to Me, all who are weary and carry heavy burdens, and I will give you rest"* (Matthew 11:28 NLT). He longs to be our hiding place, our safe space. *"He who dwells in the secret place of the Most High shall abide under the shadow of the Almighty. I will say of the Lord, 'He is my refuge and my fortress; my God, in Him I will trust"* (Psalm 91:1–2 NLT).

This is an invitation for all. It's for those who present strongly and polished. It's for the ones who have moved on or managed the pain in silence. It is for the weary, for the wounded, and for the one who is barely breathing under the weight of the pain. If you run to Him and you let Him tend to it like the Good Shepherd He is, He will pour oil and wine in your wounds, and He will speak truth to destroy lies that have been planted by the enemy throughout your life. The longer you carry it alone, the heavier it becomes. Unattended wounds attract infections, pain left unprocessed builds walls and inner vows made in traumatic moments like "I'll never let anyone hurt me like that again," or "I must've deserved it," or "God must not have cared" sends you on a pursuit of a life God never intended for you to live. Slowly, this pain becomes your posture.

But here's the beauty of grace: whether you come to Him in the moment or after a decade of delay, His arms are still open. The invitation never expires. Jesus is still standing at the door knocking (Revelation 3:20), still offering Himself as rest for the weary, still whispering, "Come." Yet the sooner you come, the softer the wound. The sooner you run, the less time pain has to shape you. So don't wait. Don't wait until you've figured out how to pray. Don't wait until the right words come. Run into His presence, messy, broken, angry, confused and real raw. God is not offended by your honesty. He's drawn to it. The invitation is not to fix yourself. It's not to explain your pain. It's simply this: Come. When it takes your breath away, come. When your eyes can't stop leaking, come. When you don't understand why it happened, come. When you're numb and have nothing to say, come. Jesus is the only one who can hold pain and still heal it. So come to the One who sees it all and loves you still. The door is open. The invitation stands. And He's waiting to bind your wounds because your trauma is not your identity.

Facing the Wounds

You cannot heal what you refuse to face. That simple truth, rooted in Ephesians 5:13—*"But everything exposed by the light becomes visible—and everything that is illuminated becomes a light"*—reminds us that God doesn't expose us to shame us. He exposes to heal us. What we keep hidden in the dark continues to fester, but what we allow His light to touch begins to mend.

It's a strange thing, really, how the human heart copes with pain. When wounds are too deep or moments too traumatic, we often respond by burying the experience beneath layers of denial, busyness, false strength, or amnesia. We tuck it so far down into the soul that years later, we find ourselves reacting with fear, anger, or insecurity, never realizing we're still bleeding from something we never allowed ourselves to look at. We call it forgetting. We call it moving on. But the truth is, it's not gone. It's just buried alive.

Let me go first. Let me show you what I had to face. When I was a teenager, I was raped at knifepoint. Thankfully, I confided in a friend, who then told her mother. That mother called mine, and my mom showed up immediately with the police. I was rushed to the hospital to ensure I was physically okay and to begin what should have been the first steps of emotional healing. The school I attended was contacted to inform them of the situation, hoping to give me space to recover. But in an unfortunate moment, my assistant principal shared what had happened in front of other students. The news spread fast. What should have remained private became public, and with it came a deep sense of shame, embarrassment, and grief. I buried the pain. I convinced myself that silence equaled strength. That if I didn't talk about it, it would eventually lose its grip on me, and for a while, I believed it had. But trauma doesn't just disappear; it waits.

Years later, my husband was trying to advocate for me in a situation and accidentally shared something with a group instead of an individual. It was an innocent mistake, but it hit me hard. In an instant, I was that young girl again. I was panicked, running through the house screaming with my children running behind me, asking what was wrong. I was exposed and undone. I found myself in a closet, shaking, weeping, and overwhelmed. It was as if all the pain I had buried had finally surfaced, and this time, it wouldn't go back underground. That moment marked the beginning of a new kind of healing for me. I couldn't bury it again. I had to face it. I began opening up to my mom about things I had held back, not to blame, but to release. I went to counseling, and when one therapist didn't feel like the right fit, I found another. I was determined to get free, and little by little, I began to feel it: lightness. Peace. Strength.

At thirty-eight, I chose to live and not just exist or not just function, but truly live. I had to live for myself, for my family, and for my God. What once was hidden in darkness had been brought into the light, and what once weighed me down now became part of my testimony. This pain didn't disqualify me. It qualified me. And now, I offer that story, not as a scar to be pitied, but as a place where God met me, healed me, and gave me purpose. Because I know what it feels like to think you've grown past something, only for it to show up again in a conversation, a memory, or even in the way you love or don't love yourself and others. God, in His mercy, has a way of bringing these hidden places to the surface, not to embarrass us, but to free us. The things we refuse to face eventually face us. But here's the beauty of it: Jesus doesn't just call us to confront our pain; He walks us through it. He stands in the middle of the memory with us, not as a harsh critic but as a compassionate Savior.

There's a phenomenon in trauma studies called repression; the brain's defense mechanism to protect us from overwhelming emotional pain. But spiritual healing calls for something deeper than protection; it calls for transformation. Transformation only happens when the wound is acknowledged, named, and surrendered. When you begin to face your wounds, details may come back slowly, sometimes through tears, sometimes in dreams, sometimes while doing something ordinary. That's not a weakness. That's your soul remembering what it needs to release. Holy Spirit, the Counselor, is gentle and precise in this work. He brings up what you are ready to face, and in His presence, even the ugliest things lose their power to define you.

I've come to learn that avoidance is not healing. Avoidance may feel like peace, but it's a counterfeit version. It may look like strength, but it's often fear in disguise. Avoiding your wounds doesn't mean they've healed. It just means they've gone into hiding. God never asked us to numb, deny, or pretend. He called us to bring it all into His presence, where light and truth live. John 8:32 NLT says, *"You will know the truth, and the truth will set you free."* But you cannot be set free by a truth you refuse to face. Psalm 147:3 NLT tells us that God heals wounds, not masks. Psalm 139:23 NLT dares us to let God search the depths of our hearts, not just the polished parts, but the raw and buried places too. There's a difference between rest and retreat. Rest is from God. Retreat is often our defense mechanism, a way of hiding behind busyness, spiritual language, or emotional walls. But God's healing doesn't live in retreat. It lives in surrender.

Avoidance keeps us emotionally immature. It pauses our growth, stunts our relationships, and delays our calling. You cannot avoid the valley and still receive what the valley was designed to teach you. Healing isn't skipping over the pain it's walking through it, hand in hand with the Lord. Ask the Lord to show you just the next step. Not the whole path. Just the next layer. Use Psalm 139:23 as your guide: *"Search me, God, and know my heart; test me and know my anxious thoughts."* Let that become your prayer: "Lord, show me what I've buried. Help me feel it, so You can heal it." Then make a declaration, a line in the sand that says you're done hiding: "I am safe with God. My healing matters. I will no longer avoid what needs to be addressed."

Avoidance isn't deliverance. It's delay. Jesus didn't come to delay your freedom. He came to finish it. You don't have to be fearless. You just have to be honest, and healing will meet you right there. The healing that was achieved on the cross over two thousand years ago. Facing your wounds is an invitation to freedom. Don't run from the mirror. Let Jesus hold it. He sees it all and still says, "You are mine." Psalm 34:18 – *"The Lord is close to the brokenhearted..."*

Trash Day: A Lesson in Letting Go

Healing isn't always loud. Sometimes, it's a quiet moment in a counseling room that forever shifts your perspective. I was in a session, recounting every painful detail I had stored away: memories, regrets, betrayals, old patterns. My counselor was walking with me through my tendency to over analyze every word I said, every conversation I had. I was stuck in a cycle of mental self-criticism, rehearsing every perceived mistake like it was a script I couldn't forget. She stopped me mid-sentence and asked, "When's your trash day?" I blinked. "Tuesdays and Fridays." She nodded and replied, "What if you never had a trash day? What if you never took the trash out? What would your house look like?" That hit me like a divine gut check. We opened to Psalm 51:10 and read it slowly together: *"Create in me a clean heart, O God; and renew a right spirit within me."* It became more than just a verse. It became my medication and security blanket when the junk in my mind started talking again.

When old, stinky memories tried to convince me I'd never be free. When my own thoughts accused me of not being enough. I knew it was time to take the trash out. But how? I thought I'd start by writing all the ugly stuff down, every memory, thought, feeling, and wound, and throw the paper away. But I felt Holy Spirit speak to me clearly: "Go get the nicest journal you have." Not just any paper. Not a scrap. A beautiful journal. One that would hurt to let go of. I went to my nightstand of journals, and there it was. It was gorgeous, leather-bound, with gold-foil letters and a verse on the front: "With God all things are possible." I had picked that journal out for dreams and destiny. I thought I'd fill it with plans, goals, prayers, and affirmations. But instead, it sat there, collecting dust. Just like me.

Suddenly, I understood. That journal represented me. Nice on the outside. Scripture written across me. Picked out for something beautiful. But inside? I was stuffed with trash: negative details of memories, negative words, and traumatic experiences. Stuff I never took out that I was carrying around as my identity. I had become like that journal, created for greatness but neglecting to let go of junk I was never meant to keep or allow to identify who I am. So, I started writing every memory, every lie, every shame-soaked thought, and every hurtful event.

Page by page, I emptied the trash, and when the journal was full, I threw it away. Not out of disrespect. But as an act of release, because I'm not my past. I'm not sure what happened. I'm not the trash. That was never my identity. It was just part of my story.

So, here's my challenge to you. Yes, you, the one reading this with a lump in your throat because you know your soul's been carrying trash for far too long. I dare you to do what I did. Find the nicest journal or notebook you have. You know the one you've been saving for something "special." Because this is special and it's holy. Begin to write down the lies, the shame, the memories that replay in your head like a broken record. The things you wish you could forget but haven't. The things that still whisper you're not enough, not wanted, not worthy, and when you're done, don't read it back. Don't analyze it or rehearse it. Just throw it out. Literally, toss it in the trash where it belongs because those things are not you. They are not your identity. They're just the old trash trying to take up space in a house God is trying to clean. Let this be your declaration: "That's not who I am anymore." The Word of God is clear about who you are: *"For we are God's masterpiece. He has created us anew in Christ Jesus, so we can do the good things He planned for us long ago."* Ephesians 2:10 (NLT)

You are a masterpiece, not a mess. You were created on purpose and for a purpose. The trash doesn't get to define you. God does, and He's calling you to rise in truth, not sit in the stink of yesterday. Let today be the day you take out the trash and never bring it back in.

The Call to Forgive

Our greatest example of forgiveness is Jesus, not in a peaceful sanctuary, but on a rugged cross, in the thick of agony, surrounded by mockers and murderers. As the blood ran down His face and the weight of our sin pressed upon His shoulders, He opened His mouth to pray: *"Father, forgive them, for they don't know what they are doing"* (Luke 23:34, NLT). That was not weakness; it was divine strength. Jesus understood the mission. He came not for the deserving, but for the broken, the blind, the prideful, the violent, the fearful, and the religious elite. The truth is, we are them and are no different, just dressed in different wounds. If it had not been for the Lord, we too would be lost and bound for a real hell that was never created for us. Thank you, Lord, for your forgiveness.

Forgiveness is more than a feeling. It is discipline, maturity, healing, and freedom. These are not optional extras; they are necessary for deep cleansing and wholeness. Forgiveness scrapes out the infection so the wound can close. It is not forgetting the offense but refusing to let it hold you captive. It says: "I know what you did. But it does not define me, and it does not control me. I am no longer tethered to the pain you caused." To forgive is to say, "I am healed, and I pray you are too." Forgiveness is an act of mercy, not just toward the offender, but toward ourselves. It gives us eyes to see, through the blood of Jesus, both them and us. It allows us to believe again in a God who is loving, just, and kind enough to transform any heart, even ours. Forgiveness is salvation. Salvation for you and potentially, salvation for the one who wronged you, if they receive it.

But let this be clear: forgiveness does not excuse the act. It doesn't dismiss the pain or erase the wrong that was done. Scripture is unflinching about the consequences of sin. Galatians 6:7 (NLT) warns, *"Don't be misled—you cannot mock the justice of God. You will always harvest what you plant."* Romans 6:23 adds, *"For the wages of sin is death..."* God is just, and every sin has a cost. What forgiveness does is shift the responsibility of justice into God's righteous hands. It is not letting someone off the hook in the sense of pretending it didn't happen; it's taking them off your hook and placing them into the hands of the only One qualified to judge rightly. Forgiveness is a declaration that "I fear the Lord more than I fear the consequences of holding on to this pain." As Proverbs 24:12 reminds us, *"He will repay all people as their actions deserve."*

Forgiveness places a holy reverence in your heart, not just toward God and His mercy, but His judgment. You stop carrying the burden of trying to punish, control, or fix what only God can. You stop drinking the poison of bitterness, hoping it affects someone else. Forgiveness leads to freedom, and freedom in Christ brings clarity of mind. When your freedom is built on Christ, not on emotions, retaliation, or false peace, you are no longer enslaved to the broken record of negative thoughts and paralyzing feelings. The constant loop of what they did and how they made you feel loses its power. Your mind, once clouded with offense, becomes guarded by the peace of God. Paul wrote in Philippians 4:7 (NLT), *"Then you will experience God's peace, which exceeds anything we can understand. His peace will guard your hearts and minds as you live in Christ Jesus."*

True freedom fills you with love that doesn't ignore truth but is rooted in it. A love that has been poured out into our hearts by the Holy Spirit (Romans 5:5). It carries you into every phase of life with grace, because you're no longer walking in reaction to your past, you're walking in revelation of who you are now: forgiven, redeemed, and whole. When we walk in forgiveness, we begin to think differently. Romans 12:2 (NLT) reminds us: *"Let God transform you into a new person by changing the way you think."* Forgiveness is not just emotional; it is a spiritual transformation. The clarity it brings aligns your thoughts with the truth of Christ, who declared, *"So if the Son sets you free, you are truly free"* (John 8:36, NLT), and when the Son sets you free, the lies of the enemy, the sting of betrayal, and the sting of guilt lose their grip. This clarity is not temporary; it is sustaining. Isaiah 26:3 (NLT) promises, *"You will keep in perfect peace all who trust in you, all whose thoughts are fixed on you."* You are no longer bound by bitterness; you are anchored by grace.

You vs. You: When Trauma Leads the Way

One of the most silent but fiercest battles we ever fight is not against the enemy, but against ourselves. It's not always spiritual warfare or demonic opposition; it's the war within our own hearts. It's you vs. you, yes, but it's also soul vs. spirit, and flesh vs. the Holy Spirit. Our soul is made up of mind, will, and emotions, and often wants comfort, validation, and control. But our spirit, when reborn in Christ, longs to submit, obey, and walk by faith. Watchman Nee, in his powerful work The Release of the Spirit, teaches that the outer man (soul and flesh) must be broken for the inner man (spirit) to be released and usable by God. This breaking is not cruelty, it's sanctification. Many never walk in true purpose because they resist this holy breaking and cling to what feels safe, familiar, or emotionally satisfying. We see this tragic tension lived out in the life of King Saul. Saul had the call, and he had the anointing. He had the people's favor and a divine assignment. But his downfall wasn't a lack of opportunity; it was his refusal to submit. Repeatedly, Saul chose his emotions over obedience, appearance over repentance, and self-preservation over surrender.

Even before Saul disobeyed God outwardly, we can see the residue of internal wounds shaping how he viewed himself and ultimately, how he responded to his calling. In 1 Samuel 9:21, Saul responds to the prophet Samuel's declaration that he is chosen by God with these words: *"But am I not a Benjamite, from the smallest tribe of Israel, and isn't my clan the least of all the clans of the tribe of Benjamin? Why do you say such a thing to me?"* (NIV). Here, Saul reveals a fractured identity rooted in trauma and limitation. His response wasn't humility; it was insecurity masquerading as humility. His entire sense of worth was filtered through the history of his tribe, the tribe of Benjamin, which had been nearly wiped out in civil war (Judges 20–21). That national shame and tribal trauma had trickled down into Saul's personal narrative. He carried that generational weight into his calling, unable to believe that God could choose someone from "the least" and do something great through them.

But here's the danger: unhealed trauma doesn't just limit how we see ourselves, it limits how we respond to God. Saul didn't just doubt himself; he doubted the God who had called him. And because his soul was so shaped by rejection, shame, and inferiority, he never fully surrendered to the Spirit's leading. He remained a man ruled by the fear of man, the need for control, and the pride of self-preservation. He built monuments to himself (1 Samuel 15:12), blamed others for his disobedience (1 Samuel 15:24), and ultimately sought guidance from darkness when he could no longer hear from the Lord (1 Samuel 28:7).

He was desperate for direction, and instead of turning to the Lord in humility, he returned to a familiar and forbidden practice by consulting a medium at Endor. That one choice to lean on the flesh instead of the Spirit, to return to what God had already forbidden, sealed his fate. His crown didn't just fall; it was forfeited. God's rejection of Saul was not sudden; it was the result of repeated resistance. The Holy Spirit had withdrawn, not because God is cruel, but because Saul had made it clear he would not be led.

Saul is no longer a new king; he's a tormented, rejected man standing in a war that seems impossible to win and a silent God that will not answer him. The Philistines are now haunting the Israelites, and from the Mount of Gilboa, Saul can see just how huge their army is. I believe he was overwhelmed. He was overwhelmed by demonic forces. There was no Holy Spirit or deliverance ministry because Jesus had not yet come. The closest thing he had to deliverance or a way to God was Samuel, and he was dead. No matter how many advisors or lots they pull to ask God if the Israelites will win or lose, God is not speaking. Saul's response is not a prayer for the mercy of God or repentance but desperation. Saul was frantic at the reality that God's rejection was manifesting. He disguises himself and seeks out a witch to summon the spirit of Samuel. The very thing he once outlawed, he now runs to. Saul defaulted to operating out of familiarity. He defaulted to what was always in his heart: his own strength, his pride, his trauma. He was on a desperate pursuit to not be the least important (his trauma from being in the tribe of Benjamin) even while being in the highest-powered position (he was already King). Why? When your trauma isn't healed, you'll always return to what's familiar.

When can we see Saul default to his trauma throughout the chapter? First, he had the wrong advisors around him. He asked his advisors to "find a woman who is a medium." These advisors were just as filled with a mixture as he was. We can determine this because they immediately responded, *"There is one at Endor."* Second, we can see Saul's heart posture show up in his actions. He disguised himself and disrobed to dress in normal everyday clothes. This act of disguising himself is really a picture of how he saw himself. He dressed how his trauma defined him. Ordinary. He dressed according to how his emotions led him. Rejected.

I saw myself in the story of Saul. Like Saul, I've wrestled with deep soul bruises. I've struggled with insecurity, rejection, grief, and abandonment. When I was drowning in pain, I turned to things that numbed me but never healed me. Alcohol, people-pleasing, and approval-chasing, to name a few. All of it gave me a temporary escape but left me emptier than before. It wasn't until I opened my heart in my most broken place and became naked and unashamed before God that I finally saw freedom. While Saul tried to cope in the dark, I ran to the Light. Here's the difference between Saul and me: Jesus. Yeshua. The One who disrobed not to hide, but to heal. The One who didn't disguise His brokenness but bore mine. Saul died bound by the familiar. I came alive because I dared to believe in something new. *"Behold, I am doing a new thing; now it springs forth..."* (Isaiah 43:19 KJV)

God is calling us out. He's calling us out of comfort, out of false identity, out of trauma-led decisions. He's calling us into Him, into wholeness, into kingdom identity and freedom, and into the deep. You don't have to disguise yourself anymore, and you don't have to keep living like what happened to you defines you. You are not what they did or what they said about you. You are His. Fearfully and wonderfully made. Seen. Known. Chosen. God is inviting you into healing that doesn't rely on the familiar but is rooted in faith.

You Have an Intercessor

In the quiet chambers of your pain, when words escape you, when the warfare is heavy, and your faith feels like it's slipping through your fingers, you are not alone. You have Someone pleading for you. Not just a sympathetic listener, but a divine Advocate. Jesus Himself, your Savior and your High Priest, is interceding for you. *"Simon, Simon, Satan has asked to sift each of you like wheat. But I have pleaded in prayer for you, Simon, that your faith should not fail."* (Luke 22:31-32 NLT) To say that Jesus pleaded in prayer for us is not to make light of a kind gesture; it is to behold a heavenly transaction. The word used in this verse carries the weight of urgent, heartfelt intercession.

Jesus was not whispering general prayers. He was standing in the gap with the full knowledge of Peter's upcoming failure, already praying for his future restoration. Before Peter denied Him, Jesus had already secured the promise that he would return not just for Himself, but to strengthen others. This is the kind of Intercessor you have. You are not being prayed for out of obligation, but out of love. Jesus sees the sifting in your life. He sees the trials, the spiritual fatigue, the warfare coming for your mind, your health, your identity, and He prays that your faith would not fail. Not that you wouldn't cry. Not that you wouldn't fall. But that your faith would hold, even when everything else feels broken, and Jesus doesn't stop there.

Even after His resurrection, He continues this ministry. *"He lives forever to intercede with God on [our] behalf"* (Hebrews 7:25). He lives to intercede for you, and His prayers didn't end with Peter. They are ongoing, active, and deeply personal. In your darkest night, in your weakest moment, Jesus is still praying, and when your words run dry, the Holy Spirit steps in. *"And the Holy Spirit helps us in our weakness... the Spirit pleads for us believers in harmony with God's own will."* (Romans 8:26-28 NLT) The Spirit doesn't need eloquence. He doesn't wait for perfect posture or polished sentences. He meets us in the groaning, in the aching, in the holy silence. The Spirit pleads with divine alignment to the will of God, praying what we can't articulate, interpreting the language of our tears, our fatigue, our buried grief. You are being prayed for on every level by the Son before the Father and by the Spirit within your heart.

Sometimes, that intercession doesn't come through words at all. Sometimes it flows through tears. When the Spirit prays through you, it's not always in sentences; it's in sighs, groans, and streams of tears that Heaven knows how to interpret. Tears are not a weakness; they are a prayer technology. They bypass flesh and intellect and go straight into the courts of Heaven. *"You keep track of all my sorrows. You have collected all my tears in your bottle..."* (Psalm 56:8 NLT). God collects them because they speak. Your tears are not a mess to be cleaned up—they are intercession. They carry a weight that words often cannot. They are language, worship, and they are warfare.

For me, tears did not come easily. I've never been one to cry, especially not in front of people. Vulnerability felt too risky. Too exposed. There are only a handful of times I can recall crying in front of anyone, including my husband. I was the strong one. The composed one. If tears ever escaped, it was when I was extremely angry and more often during worship or in the sanctuary when God's presence felt safe enough to let the walls down. But even then, I was quick to wipe them away, to apologize for them, to ask, "Why am I crying?" During my healing process, that all began to shift.

I remember walking to my office one day after praying. I had poured my heart out but still felt restrained in a way I couldn't fully explain. Then I heard the Holy Spirit whisper gently, but clearly: "Cry. Your tears speak a language that words cannot." That moment unlocked something in me. It was as if Heaven had been waiting not for a perfectly worded prayer, but for a release. My tears, once seen as a sign of weakness, suddenly felt like keys. Keys that opened healing, intercession, and the very presence of God. The Lord reminded me that He treasures every tear. He bottles them, not because they're sentimental, but because they're sacred. They are prayers that say what I can't and fight for what I don't know how to fight. Your tears, beloved, are not wasted. They reach where language fails, and they intercede when your strength has collapsed. Crying doesn't mean you're falling apart; it means your spirit is speaking in a holy language that moves the heart of God.

The language of the Spirit includes more than words. It includes tears, moanings, groanings, tongues, and utterances birthed from deep within. These aren't chaos, they're code. Divine keys. Spiritual downloads. Like encrypted software, they release Heaven's responses, healing, direction, and divine instruction. In your surrender, Heaven speaks.

Above every groan, every tear, every whisper of pain, there is a voice still speaking: the voice of the blood of Jesus. *"You have come… to Jesus, the mediator of a new covenant, and to the sprinkled blood, which speaks a better word than the blood of Abel."* (Hebrews 12:24 NLT) His blood speaks. It speaks louder than trauma and guilt. Louder than betrayal, loss, or warfare. The blood of Jesus cries out on your behalf with mercy, with justice, with redemption. It silences the accusations of the enemy and settles the matter in Heaven's court. So yes, cry, groan, and pray in the Spirit and let your heart rest in this eternal truth: Jesus is still interceding. Not just with temporary words, but with eternal blood. His intercession didn't end on the cross; it lives on through the throne, and that blood is still enough. You have an Intercessor. You are not alone, and His blood still speaks for you.

Reflection
- What's your invitation?
- Who or what has God used to pull you closer to healing?
- Who has loved you even when you weren't at your best?
- Where is God gently knocking and asking to come in, not to judge, but to restore?

Prophetic Declaration of Healing

I declare that I am no longer defined by my wounds, my past, or my pain. Jesus, the Healer, has invited me into His presence, and I say yes to His call. I open the door of my heart to Him, and I will not hide in fear, shame, or avoidance. Every hidden place in me is being flooded with His light, and what once brought me torment is becoming a testimony of His grace.

I declare that I am not abandoned. I am loved, chosen, and covered. The love of God is my shelter, my refuge, and my peace.

The lies of the enemy are silenced by the blood of Jesus, which speaks a better word over me: mercy, freedom, and redemption.

I declare that I will face my wounds with courage, knowing I am safe in the presence of God. What was buried is being brought into the light for my healing, not my shame. I release every weight of unforgiveness, bitterness, and fear into the hands of the Righteous Judge.

I forgive, because I am forgiven. I release, because I am released.

I declare that I will no longer live by trauma or familiarity. I will no longer dress myself in rejection, shame, or fear. I am clothed in righteousness, wrapped in grace, and anointed with purpose. I am a masterpiece, created anew in Christ Jesus for good works that He prepared in advance for me.

I declare that Jesus is my constant Intercessor, and the Holy Spirit prays through me. Even my tears are worship, and every cry of my soul is heard in Heaven. I am never alone, for the Lord is close to the brokenhearted and He binds up every wound.

Today, I say yes to the standing invitation of healing. I collapse into His arms, where rest is promised and peace is preserved. I am free, I am whole, and I am His. In Jesus' mighty name. Amen.

Chapter 5

The Roots that Hurt

Left unchecked, trauma doesn't just sit in your history; it bleeds into your habits. It chooses your relationships. It governs your theology. It alters how you pray, trust, and lead. We start making choices through the lens of self-protection, not Holy Spirit conviction. This is why Scripture warns, *"The heart is deceitful above all things... who can know it?"* (Jeremiah 17:9).

Trauma might've chosen for you in the past, but truth can choose for you now. Imagine a fruit tree that looks beautiful on the outside, with lush leaves, decent fruit, and standing tall. But underneath the surface, something is off. The roots are decaying. Maybe they were planted in poor soil. Maybe they've been invaded by pests. Maybe a storm beat down so hard that the tree never recovered its stability. Whatever the cause, the truth is this: no matter how much fruit the tree tries to bear, if the root is sick, the fruit will suffer. The root is where nourishment flows. It's where stability begins. And in our spiritual and emotional lives, our "roots" are formed through early experiences, words spoken over us, family dynamics, traumas, and patterns we learned to survive. Some of us have roots tangled in rejection, never chosen, always overlooked. Others have roots scarred by abuse, betrayal, abandonment, or fear. These roots don't just stay buried; they grow up into our fruit: our attitudes, our reactions, our choices in relationships, how we view God, and even how we see ourselves.

Trauma to the root shows up in different ways. A root bound in rejection might produce a fruit of perfectionism, always trying to earn love. A root damaged by betrayal might bear the fruit of mistrust or isolation. A root infected by shame can show up in how we sabotage good things because deep down, we don't feel worthy of them. Like root rot in a tree, these unseen wounds begin to poison everything above the surface. But here's the powerful truth: before God heals the fruit, He exposes the root. Why? Because He's not in the business of superficial healing. He doesn't just want to polish your leaves or repaint your bark. He wants to make you whole from the inside out. That means digging deep, revealing what's been hidden, and lovingly pulling up what's been killing you slowly, and once it's exposed, Jesus doesn't leave us in our pain. He uproots it. He tears down what the enemy planted and replaces it with what is holy, true, and life-giving.

This chapter is your invitation to look beneath the surface. To let the Spirit walk you back through the garden of your life and examine what's been buried but still alive. To realize that Jesus is not afraid of your roots. In fact, it's His specialty. He is the master gardener, and He knows how to replant you in healing soil. As Isaiah 61:3 says, He gives "beauty for ashes," and makes us into "oaks of righteousness, a planting of the Lord for the display of His splendor." Healing starts at the root—and with God, nothing hidden is beyond His reach.

Unhealed trauma is an open door

Trauma is not a demon. It is a soul wound. But left untreated, trauma becomes a doorway, a breach in the soul's defenses that invites demonic interference. Trauma doesn't possess you, but it can position you for bondage if not healed through Christ. As a student at Cultivate University, my mentor, Apostle Torace Solomon, teaches this with clarity and conviction in his book Finger of God. He writes, "Demons don't just enter where they want. They enter through openings, and trauma, especially unhealed trauma, becomes an open door." This truth changed how I saw my own story. Trauma could be the belief that you're unlovable. The invisible grip of fear when love gets too close. The shrinking back in leadership because past rejection told you not to speak up. These aren't just emotional quirks; they're spiritual agreements. "Demons cannot torment you without access, and they often gain access through life events that left you wounded. They build their case on your pain." (Finger of God, Solomon) In other words, trauma is the wound, the lie becomes the infection, and the demon becomes the squatter.

The Greek word from which we derive trauma is τραῦμα (TRAH-oo-mah - trauma), and it literally means "wound" or "damage." In classical Greek usage, it referred to a physical injury or wound to the body. Over time, especially in medical and psychological contexts, the term expanded to include emotional or psychological wounds that leave lasting effects on the mind and soul. So, when we say "trauma," even in modern conversation, we are using a term that historically and linguistically means a wound and not a sin, not a demon, but a real place of injury in the human experience.

This makes Luke 10:34 especially powerful, where the Good Samaritan "went to him and bandaged his wounds [traumata], pouring on oil and wine." It's a picture of Jesus as the one who tends to our trauma by not ignoring it but healing it." Biblically, we see the concept of soul wounds reflected in Psalm 147:3: "He heals the brokenhearted and binds up their wounds." This is not a metaphor; it is a ministry. Trauma disrupts our sense of safety, worth, and identity. It fractures the heart and opens the mind to lies the enemy is eager to whisper. That's why we cannot ignore trauma in the Church or anywhere. Jesus didn't just cast out demons; He healed broken people. He touched the places others avoided. Solomon teaches: "Deliverance is not a substitute for healing, and healing is not a substitute for deliverance. Some need both. Healing addresses the wound; deliverance removes the squatter." Trauma is not your fault, but partnering with Jesus for truth, wholeness, and freedom to be healed is your responsibility.

Healing Is Your Responsibility

It's not someone else's job to make you whole. Healing begins the moment you stop waiting for others to fix what they never had the power to heal. Scripture reminds us in Galatians 5:1 (NLT), *"It is for freedom that Christ has set us free. Stand firm, then, and do not let yourselves be burdened again by a yoke of slavery."* When you attach your healing to another person's behavior, apology, consistency, or validation, you become enslaved to outcomes that only God can control. This creates emotional bondage for both you and them. You are not free, because your sense of peace is tethered to someone else's performance. And they are not free, because they feel the unspoken pressure to become what only Jesus was meant to be.

Healing is your responsibility, not anyone else's. Galatians 6:5 says, *"Each one should carry their own load."* While others can walk with you, pray for you, and encourage you, they cannot carry what only you and Christ are designed to handle. When you expect your spouse, friends, leaders, or even your counselor to love you in all the ways you were never loved or include you in all the places you once felt excluded, you set yourself and them up for failure. You end up placing expectations on mere humans that only God was ever meant to fulfill. Jeremiah 17:5 warns us, *"Cursed is the one who trusts in man, who draws strength from mere flesh and whose heart turns away from the Lord."* When you lean too heavily on people, your heart will eventually drift from the Source of true strength.

There are signs that may reveal you've unknowingly placed your healing in someone else's hands. You may find yourself stuck, unable to move forward because you're still waiting for an apology. Your peace may rise or fall based on how someone else acts. You might constantly replay what they did, hoping one day they'll realize their wrong and fix it. You may even catch yourself making new relationships pay the price for old wounds, expecting them to overperform to soothe hurts they never caused. These patterns are not healing; they're signs of misplaced trust.

Healing is not about denial, nor is it about blaming yourself. It's about reclaiming your authority in Christ. It's about choosing to release the burden of "what they didn't do" and embracing what God already did. Jesus is the only one strong enough, perfect enough, and willing enough to carry the weight of your brokenness. When you look to Him, you find healing that is not delayed by someone else's failure to repent. You find freedom that doesn't hinge on someone else getting it right. Your healing starts when you take your eyes off them and fix them on Him.

I want to challenge you to actively shift the weight of your healing from yourself and anyone else to God. Here's how first, who have you expected to "make it right" before you heal? Write their names down, even if you are included. Write it out. Next, write "I release you" by each name and pray this simple prayer: "God, I give You back the power I gave to them. I take responsibility for my healing today." Then take a moment to journal this: "What would it look like if I no longer waited on someone to make me whole?"

Healing is between you and God. Not you and "them." It's not fair to you, and it's not fair to them, to carry what only Christ can carry. Release them and reclaim your power. Healing is your responsibility, but freedom is God's gift. And here's the most freeing part: once you take responsibility, you don't have to carry it alone. You were never designed to heal in your own strength. You are called to participate in your healing but not to perform for it. The weight of your wholeness was always meant to rest on God's shoulders, not yours. So, shift it. Hand it over. Healing may start with your yes, but it is sustained by His grace. Let the same God who saved you also restore you. The burden is too heavy for you, but it's never been too heavy for Him. Let Jesus carry what you can't. Let Him finish what He started.

The Long Reach of Rejection

Rejection isn't just a moment or a memory; it becomes a lens. A distorted filter that warps how we view ourselves, others, and even God. When rejection is left unhealed, it doesn't sit quietly in the corner of our hearts. It lingers, leaks, and leads. It colors every room we enter and whispers through every relationship we hold dear. But even deeper than that, rejection is not just emotional, it's spiritual. It's warfare. It is a demonic wound that attacks the very core of our identity.

For me, the seeds of rejection weren't planted in loud or obvious moments. My father never outright told me he didn't want me. But silence can speak, absence can shout, and inconsistency can cut deeper than words ever could. After my parents divorced when I was ten, we moved from Call to Houston. Although I knew my father was sometimes in the city, he never came to see me. He didn't try. He didn't show up. And so, rejection crept in. Not because of what he said, but because of what he didn't do.

The pain wasn't just mine. I watched my two older brothers wrestle with their own father wounds, each of them feeling the abandonment. I never asked, "Why didn't you come?" or "Why didn't you try?" I never blamed him. I just held it quietly, almost nobly, as if minimizing the pain made me more healed. But what we don't confront eventually confronts us and rejection has a long reach.

I didn't recognize the wound until I found myself reaching for approval from another man who was my pastor. I wanted his yes, and I craved his affirmation. I even went around my own husband's leading to chase the nod of a spiritual leader, not just once, but I lived in this state. This one time when that approval didn't come, I spiraled. My counselor helped me see that I had broken God's order. She reminded me that my husband's no was God's protection, and I was wrong to bypass his authority to feed a spiritual hunger rooted in emotional rejection.

At the same time, I took on the task of managing my dad's healthcare. He was in a facility close to my home, and I would visit him daily. After rehabilitating, he wanted to move back home, and so he did. But suddenly, he disappeared. He wouldn't answer the phone, and he didn't call. There was no explanation, and just like that, the ache came back. It was as if the old wound reopened with a sharper edge. I wondered if he was mad at me, if I had done something wrong, if maybe he just didn't want me again. Rejection echoed in every unanswered ring. Here's the part that's hardest to admit: I brought that same wound into my relationship with God and into my worship. The Holy Spirit was revealing that when I lifted my hands during church, it was not just in praise but in a subconscious cry for validation. One day, as I was "worshiping", I heard the Holy Spirit whisper, "Are you lifting your hands to encourage the worship team, or to worship Me?" Ouch. Truth pierced me. I was serving hard, worshiping loudly, and giving much, but from the wrong place. I wasn't being led by the Spirit. I was being led by the need to be seen, accepted, and affirmed.

This is what rejection does when it goes undetected. It hijacks your purpose and morphs pure worship into performance. It dismisses the quiet, loving voice of the Father and replaces it with a chasing after applause, affirmation, and appreciation. But God. In the middle of my unraveling, God met me. He whispered, "I am your Father." He didn't shout. He didn't rebuke. He reminded. "I am Abba." That's when I built a spiritual altar in my heart. Not of stone or wood but of surrender. That He, my Heavenly Father, was always present, always faithful, and always enough. He didn't need to prove it with flowers or visits or phone calls. His presence was my proof. His Word is my affirmation. His Son, Jesus, is the seal of my acceptance.

Romans 8:15 says, *"So you have not received a spirit that makes you fearful slaves. Instead, you received God's Spirit when He adopted you as His own children. Now we call him, 'Abba, Father.'"* The wound of rejection loses its grip when we rest in the truth of our adoption. You don't have to live like an orphan when Heaven has already called you daughter or son. You don't have to perform when Abba already approves. You don't have to beg for acceptance when you've already been chosen. Rejection may have reached far, but God's love reaches further. There's no wound too deep that His identity can't heal. But here's what we must also understand: Rejection is a demonic wound. It is not just emotional; it is spiritual warfare against your identity. It is the enemy's subtle yet strategic attempt to separate you from the truth of who you are in Christ and the love that has already been secured for you. Rejection is not passive; it is planned. The enemy doesn't simply hope you feel unloved; he sows schemes. He orchestrates moments, disappointments, and silences that press into your insecurities and lie to you about who you are and how God sees you.

The enemy knows that if he can distort your identity, he can distract your destiny. If he can convince you that God's love is conditional, fragile, or distant, he can make you doubt the very foundation of your faith. So, he builds brick by brick rejection from a parent, dismissal from a leader, betrayal from a friend, and with every layer, he hopes to build a wall so thick that even the truth of God's Word can't break through. But he underestimates the power of God. This war is not something we can win on our own strength. We cannot positively think our way out of it or numb ourselves through distraction. We cannot cover it with good works or mask it with the applause and affirmation of others. Rejection is not merely emotional; it is spiritual. It's not just a feeling; it's fruit. According to the spiritual warfare teaching in Strongman's His Name... What's His Game? by Drs. Jerry and Carol Robeson, rejection is one of the manifesting fruits of the strongman spirit of heaviness. That means rejection does not stand alone; it is backed by a demonic hierarchy that seeks to overwhelm the soul with grief, sorrow, despair, and spiritual fatigue. The spirit of heaviness comes to cloak the believer in darkness, and rejection is often one of its most effective tools to disconnect us from the revelation of God's love.

Deliverance, then, is not optional; it is necessary. The spirit of rejection must be confronted spiritually. We begin by coming out of agreement with it, renouncing the lie that we are unwanted, unloved, or unworthy. We repent for believing that God is like man, that He will leave when we fail, and that we must earn His affection. We cancel every word curse, emotional contract, and soul tie that has empowered this lie to stay. As Jesus declared in Matthew 18:18, *"Truly I tell you, whatever you bind on earth will be bound in heaven, and whatever you loose on earth will be loosed in heaven."* So, we bind the strongman, the spirit of heaviness, and command every fruit of rejection, fear, abandonment, and self-hate to go in Jesus' name. Then we loose the truth. We loose the garment of praise for the spirit of heaviness (Isaiah 61:3). We loose the Spirit of adoption, the love of the Father, the love of Christ, and the peace of God that guards our hearts and minds.

True deliverance doesn't end with casting something out. We must invite Someone in. We ask the Holy Spirit to fill every place where rejection once sat like a king on the throne of our identity. We ask the Father to plant His truth deep into the soil of our hearts: that we are loved, chosen, redeemed, and sealed. Not because we performed, but because He predestined us to be His before the foundation of the world. His love doesn't shift with our behavior. His love is not moody or mechanical. It is perfect. It is unfailing. It is eternal.

"See what great love the Father has lavished on us, that we should be called children of God! And that is what we are!" —1 John 3:1 *"You did not choose me, but I chose you..."* —John 15:16 *"We love because He first loved us."* —1 John 4:19

Rejection is evicted by revelation. When we believe what the blood of Jesus declares that we are accepted in the Beloved (Ephesians 1:6), then rejection loses its power. The Spirit of Truth dismantles every lying spirit. What once felt like abandonment becomes the backdrop for adoption. You are not just delivered, you are established. Not just free but filled. Not just healed but whole. *"I have loved you with an everlasting love. With unfailing love I have drawn you to myself."* — Jeremiah 31:3

Rejection tells you that love must be earned. But the cross tells you that love was already given. Rejection tells you that if you mess up, you'll be cast aside. But Scripture declares, *"Even when we are faithless, He remains faithful"* (2 Timothy 2:13). Rejection says God will leave you like others have. But Romans 8 roars back: *"I am convinced that nothing can ever separate us from God's love."* Not death. Not failure. Not abandonment. Not even rejection itself. This is how we fight back: not by striving, but by standing. Standing on the Word, standing in worship, and standing under the covering of Christ's finished work. Rejection loses its power when we embrace our adoption. *"God decided in advance to adopt us into His own family by bringing us to Himself through Jesus Christ. This is what He wanted to do, and it gave Him great pleasure."* —Ephesians 1:5 You are not tolerated. You are chosen. You are not an afterthought. You were planned. You are not forgotten. You are deeply known and fully seen. The enemy wants to distort the purity of God's love, but Christ came to restore it. When you know how deeply you are loved, rejection may knock, but it won't reside. Your identity is not based on man's opinion; it is sealed in the blood of Jesus.

Relationship Reviews: When Pain Picks for You

Trauma doesn't just leave wounds; it creates patterns. And those patterns become familiar. If we're not careful, we'll start calling familiar pain "normal" simply because it feels like home. Trauma subtly trains us in relationships how to receive love, how to give it, how to guard against it, and even how to sabotage it. It governs the kind of relationships we accept, neglect, tolerate, and invite into our lives. I didn't realize it at the time, but the way I loved, the way I feared, the friendships I chased, and even the leaders I submitted to were shaped by wounds I hadn't acknowledged. Trust violated in childhood laid a foundation for tolerating manipulation in adulthood. What I called loyalty was often just fear of being abandoned again.

Have you ever bonded with someone over trauma, only to later find out that they are unhealthy and cause chaos in your life? Until you let the Holy Spirit examine the roots of those patterns, you'll keep eating the same bitter fruit and wondering why healing feels delayed. Jesus said, *"Every plant that my heavenly Father has not planted will be pulled up by the roots"* (Matthew 15:13). Trauma opened doors for some things to be planted in you that God didn't. Things like your ideas about love, trust, worth, and boundaries. These things that were shaped in the fire of survival and not in the light of His Word. Jeremiah 17:9 warns us, *"The heart is deceitful above all things and desperately wicked; who can know it?"* That means we can't always trust what feels right, especially if our "right" was trained in dysfunction.

Many of our past decisions weren't conscious; they were trauma-led. You didn't sit down and plan to tolerate emotional neglect. But when your nervous system was trained in fear, when your soul was conditioned by abandonment, trauma started choosing for you. Trauma wears the disguise of discernment, but it is really distrust. It looks like strength, but it's self-protection. Unhealed emotional neglect governs our relational responses. We either fight, flee, freeze, or fawn when engaging in relationships that are triggers for us. These are not personality traits; they are survival mechanisms. You don't choose them; they are developed in traumatic moments. While they may have helped you survive a storm, they cannot help you build a life. We must surrender them, bring them into the light, and not bury them deeper. In the hands of God, even your trauma responses can become testimonies. It's time to let truth lead instead. *"Then you will know the truth, and the truth will set you free"* (John 8:32).

You may not always stop the trigger, but by the power of God's Word, you can choose a different response. That's healing. Not perfection, but participation. Healing is agreeing with God about what's true even when your feelings scream otherwise. You begin to recognize that you don't have to fight to be seen, flee when things get close, freeze when responsibility arises, or fawn to stay accepted. You are loved. You are safe. You are whole in Christ. You are healed, even if you are still healing.

Reflection: "Heal the Root, Redeem the Fruit"

Father, today I look beneath the leaves. I acknowledge that trauma is a wound, not my identity. Unhealed places have shaped patterns, and patterns have shaped choices. I have called self-protection wisdom when it was really fear. I have chased affirmation to soothe rejection. I have tolerated what felt familiar and called it normal.

Jesus, You are the Good Samaritan who tends wounds with oil and wine. You are the Master Gardener who refuses cosmetic fixes. You expose roots to heal fruit. I agree with You. I will not outsource my healing to apologies, outcomes, or people. I take responsibility to partner with Your truth. Where rejection trained my reactions, adoption will train my responses. Where heaviness pressed on my soul, the garment of praise will clothe me. Where lies built strongholds, Your Word becomes my blueprint for freedom.

Search my heart, Holy Spirit. Uproot every belief that says I am unwanted, unsafe, or unseen. Replant me in Your love. Let Galatians 5:1 anchor my will, Psalm 147:3 steady my emotions, and John 8:32 govern my choices. I choose wholeness at the root so that righteousness can show in the fruit.

Prophetic Declaration: "Rooted, Healed, Established"

Place a hand over your heart and speak this out loud.

1. I am a planting of the Lord, established as an oak of righteousness. My roots go down into Christ, and I bear good fruit by the Spirit.

2. I come out of agreement with rejection, shame, abandonment, fear, and self-protection. I renounce every lie that says I must earn love or perform for belonging.

3. By the authority of Jesus, I shut every open door created by unhealed trauma. I bind the spirit of heaviness and every fruit of rejection, and I loose the Spirit of adoption, joy, peace, and holy confidence.

4. I take responsibility for my healing. I release every person I have waited on to make me whole. My heart is anchored in the Father's love.

5. My nervous system is discipled by truth. I will not fight to be seen, flee from closeness, freeze under pressure, or fawn for approval. I respond with courage, clarity, and covenant love.

6. The Lord searches and heals my roots. Every plant not planted by my Father is pulled up, and every good root is strengthened and nourished.

7. I forgive quickly, repent boldly, and receive freely. I choose truth over triggers, presence over performance, and purpose over patterns.

8. I am chosen, adopted, and accepted in the Beloved. Nothing can separate me from the love of God in Christ Jesus.

9. My household will taste the fruit of healed roots. Peace, purity, and praise dwell here.

10. From this day forward, my life becomes a living testimony: healed at the root, holy in the fruit, and whole by the grace of God.

Chapter 6

The Unburdened Heart

Healing is not easy. If you've made it this far in the journey, then you've probably already bumped into some uncomfortable truths. Things you didn't want to feel, things you didn't want to face. The kind of truths that make you want to slam the book shut, slap a smile on your face, and say, "I'm fine. I've forgiven. I've moved on." But let's be honest, sometimes what we call "moving on" is just deflection dressed up as spiritual maturity.

Deflection may protect your image, but it starves your soul. It convinces you that appearing strong is safer than being seen as struggling, so you smile when you want to scream, serve when you need support, and perform when you should be processing. Deflection is a subtle self-betrayal. It trains you to prioritize how others perceive you over what your soul actually needs. It whispers that honesty is too risky and that vulnerability is weakness, but in doing so, it isolates you from the very grace that could restore you. You become skilled at managing impressions while silently bleeding inside, disconnected from your own emotions and distant from the God who longs to meet you in truth. Over time, this avoidance of pain doesn't just delay healing. It only deepens the wound because what you refuse to feel, you also refuse to heal. It's easier to ignore what hurts than to sit with it. Easier to quote Scripture than to apply it to our open wounds. Easier to perform strength than to admit weakness. But here's the truth: healing requires honesty. Not the kind of churchy honesty that hides behind clichés or filtered testimonies but gut-wrenching, soul-baring, snot-crying honesty.

Jesus, the Son of God, did not bypass pain. He embraced it. He wept over death. He groaned in Gethsemane. He cried out on the cross. His strength was not in emotional silence but in emotional surrender. The life of Jesus was marked not by avoidance, but by a deep willingness to feel, to carry, and to suffer for the sake of love. He was rejected by the very people He grew up around. His hometown dismissed Him, saying, *"Isn't this the carpenter's son?"* (Matthew 13:55), unable to see the Messiah in someone so familiar. The religious leaders, the ones who should've recognized Him most, plotted against Him because His truth disrupted their traditions. He fasted for forty days in the wilderness, denying Himself physical nourishment and comfort so that He could stand firm in spiritual identity and authority. Though He had every right to reign in royal luxury, He chose the path of humility, wandering without a home, healing the sick, touching the unclean, and sleeping under stars rather than palace ceilings.

In the garden of Gethsemane, He was so grieved that Scripture says His soul was *"crushed with grief to the point of death"* (Matthew 26:38 NLT), and His sweat became like drops of blood. An agony so intense it revealed the full weight of what He was about to endure. When He asked His closest friends to watch and pray with Him, they fell asleep not once, but three times. It grieved Him deeply not because He needed their power, but because He longed for their presence and support. In His humanity, He desired the comfort of companionship, and it pierced Him that those He had poured into could not stay awake with Him in His greatest moment of sorrow. On the cross, with nails piercing His hands and lungs gasping for air, He still served, even with His very last breath. He forgave the thief beside Him, He entrusted His mother to John, and He pleaded for forgiveness for His executioners. Jesus didn't escape pain, but He redeemed it. He met it head-on with love, proving that surrender in suffering is not weakness; it's divine strength. He felt deeply, so we could heal fully.

So why do we think our tears disqualify us from healing? Why do we equate feeling with failure? Numbness isn't healing. It's just pain on pause. Sooner or later, that pause will end with an outburst, a breakdown, or a silent drift away from God and people. Stuffing your emotions doesn't sanctify you; it only suffocates what God is trying to heal. You cannot heal what you refuse to feel. This chapter is an invitation to lay it all down. To unburden your heart and stop pretending you're okay. This is where the process gets messy. But this is also where grace shows up. Not the kind of grace that makes excuses for your pain, but the kind that sits with you in it and slowly lifts the weight you were never meant to carry.

Anxiety Powered by Perfection

This section sits heavily in my life. Somewhere along the way, the need to be perfect took over me. It wasn't just a character trait, but it became a form of bondage. It paralyzed me in more ways than I realized, and even now, it still tries to show up in my life, especially my relationships. I didn't understand then that my perfectionism wasn't just about having high standards or being responsible. It was powered by anxiety. Every conversation I had lived in my head for days and sometimes for years. I would replay every inflection of my voice and theirs, analyzing body language, tone, and word choice. I'd ask myself, do they think differently of me now? Did I say too much? Was I too strong, or too soft? I'd feel completely exposed, but I wouldn't say any of this out loud. Being confrontational didn't fit my image of "perfect." I had to be agreeable, easy to work with, lovable, and all the things people would describe as "good." I thought I was being strong, but the truth is, I was trying to control every variable. The painful reality is, I had no control, not then and not ever. I was living in a delusion.

My healing didn't begin in isolation but in community. God strategically positioned me around people who were just like me, but unlike me; they weren't afraid to be honest. They created safe spaces around safe people to be able to say what they felt, they named what hurt them, and without fear of judgment or the ruin of their image. I was appalled and yet deeply intrigued. Could people really live that free? I wanted that. I wanted that level of emotional honesty and spiritual security. I had spent nearly 40 years bound to anxiety disguised as perfection, and it's taken the last three years for God to begin peeling back the layers. I've explored experiences where it could have started, and more importantly, God has shown me how to move forward.

I've taken real steps toward freedom. My prayer and worship time became a sacred place of unmasking. I learned to open my heart up to friends who weren't afraid to take off their own masks. I continue to sit with a God-filled, professional counselor who helped me untangle truth from trauma. Through this journey, I've come to realize that anxiety doesn't always come from external chaos. It often comes from internal control. The belief that if I can do everything right, nothing will go wrong is a lie. One planted by the enemy because of the need to be perfect and reinforced by fear. But what if I don't get it right? What if I fail? Then anxiety steps in like a fire alarm, sounding off at every thought, every mistake, every social interaction. Philippians 4:6 tells me, *"Be anxious for nothing, but in everything by prayer and supplication with thanksgiving let your requests be made known unto God."* That's not just about calming down; it's about surrendering control and coming into agreement with God's peace.

Fear, perfectionism, and anxiety work together in a toxic cycle. They keep the mind restless and the heart heavy. But 2 Timothy 1:7 is clear: *"For God hath not given us the spirit of fear; but of power, and of love, and of a sound mind."* Fear is not from God, and if He didn't give it to me, I have no obligation to keep it. What He did give is power, love, and a sound mind. One day, I received the revelation that he gave me Power, the Holy Spirit, because Acts 1:8 says, *"But ye shall receive power, after that the Holy Ghost is come upon you."* He gave me Love, God, because 1 John 4:8 says, *"But anyone who does not love does not know God, for God is love."* A sound mind, Jesus, because Isaiah 26:3 declares, *"Thou wilt keep him in perfect peace, whose mind is stayed on thee: because he trusteth in thee."* This is the fullness of what God has given, and everything fear tries to steal.

Fear is a thief. It's not neutral, and it's not passive. John 10:10 reveals its origin: *"The thief cometh not, but for to steal, and to kill, and to destroy: I am come that they might have life, and that they might have it more abundantly."* That fear that crippled me for decades wasn't just a feeling; it was a demonic assignment. An assignment meant to rob me of my peace, my relationships, my voice, and my joy. But Jesus came to give me life, and not just any life, an abundant life. That abundance doesn't come through performance but through God's presence. It comes through grace, through truth, and through surrender.

Now I ask myself, where am I still trying to be perfect instead of being present? I recognize those old scripts, or I like to say, the negative reel, constantly playing the internal "I musts." I must keep it together. I must not fail. I must be agreeable. But those were fear-driven, not faith-driven. God has helped me rewrite them in truth. I no longer wake up trying to earn approval. I start my day speaking the Word: I have power, love, and a sound mind. His grace is enough for me. Healing is happening in the letting go. The more I surrender, the more I see that God never asked me to be flawless. He asked me to trust Him. So, I remind myself often to breathe, exhale, and inhale because the pressure I carried all those years was never from Him.

Not for My Shame, But for His Glory

My very first message was titled "Not for My Shame, But for His Glory," and that wasn't just a sermon; it was my story. Every trial, every failure, every wilderness I walked through wasn't meant to expose me for ridicule, but it was meant to glorify God. Just as Jesus said about the man born blind, *"This happened so the power of God could be seen in him"* (John 9:3 NLT), my life, and yours, is not just a series of personal battles; it's a stage for God's glory to be revealed. When we don't recognize that truth, when we fail to see that our pain has a Kingdom purpose, we begin to turn inward, and we try to carry what was meant to be surrendered. Then, before we know it, pain breeds pride. This pride is not always the loud, boastful kind. Pride can also be quiet and polished. Sometimes it sounds like, "I'm fine." Sometimes it looks like, "I don't need help," but underneath the silence is shame. Shame says, if they really knew me, they'd leave. Pride answers, Then I'll only show them what's acceptable and just like that, shame becomes the engine and pride becomes the armor. It feels like strength, but it's really self-protection rooted in unworthiness. Often, that protection wears the clothes of false humility.

False humility whispers, "I'm just trying to stay low. I don't want to be seen," but what it really means is, "If I stay invisible, I can't be rejected." It's not holiness, it's fear dressed in spiritual language. Paul warned in Colossians 2:18 against pious self-denial that looks righteous but is fueled by pride, and that's the deception: false humility is still self-centered. It keeps the attention on what I'm not, what I can't do, why I'm not enough, rather than focusing on who God is and what He has said. It binds us in the very shame that Jesus broke on the cross.

Sometimes false humility doesn't speak; it performs. It shows up as the one who gets things done first, the one who jumps in before anyone else can raise their hand. While it looks like responsibility, it's often fear that says, "If someone else does this well, there might not be room for me." I never said it out loud, but the truth was, I believed I had to be the one. I had to finish it first, do it right, and not leave space for someone else, because if they could do it too, then maybe I was never really needed. That's not humility. That's hidden insecurity masked as excellence. That's the fear of being unwanted, fueling a performance to prove worth.

But God never called us to perform for value. He called us to rest in identity. Hebrews 4:16 says, *"So let us come boldly to the throne of our gracious God. There we will receive his mercy, and we will find grace to help us when we need it most."* Real humility doesn't shrink in fear; it surrenders in faith. It doesn't deflect praise or run from calling; it reflects all glory back to the One who gave it. Jesus didn't die so you could pretend to be humble. He died so you could live free. Free from shame, free from the lies, and free from the fear of being seen. If we're honest, many of us have confused fear with reverence. We've called it holiness, but really, it was terror in disguise. We thought we were honoring God by shrinking back, but that wasn't reverence. That was shame. That was the fear of punishment, not the awe of His presence. 1 John 4:18 makes it clear: *"Such love has no fear, because perfect love expels all fear. If we are afraid, it is for fear of punishment, and this shows that we have not fully experienced his perfect love"* (NLT). God is not looking for slaves who flinch when He speaks. He's looking for sons and daughters who draw near in love, not run away in guilt. Reverence is not rooted in the fear of being destroyed; it's rooted in the wonder of being chosen. Hebrews 12:28 tells us to *"worship God acceptably with reverence and awe,"* but that reverence is birthed in the security of grace, not in the terror of condemnation. It's the holy awareness that we are standing before a righteous God and yet He calls us His own. That kind of reverence doesn't push you away; it pulls you closer. Fear says, "Don't mess up or He'll leave you." Reverence says, "He loves me too much to let me stay the same." Fear produces hiding, like Adam and Eve in the garden (Genesis 3:10), but reverence produces surrender, like Isaiah, who cried, *"Woe is me"* (Isaiah 6:5), not because he feared rejection, but because he had encountered glory. Romans 8:15 reminds us, *"So you have not received a spirit that makes you fearful slaves. Instead, you received God's Spirit when he adopted you as his own children. Now we call him, 'Abba, Father'"* (NLT). That's the difference between religious fear and redemptive reverence: one makes you run from God, the other makes you fall at His feet and call Him Father.

Make no mistake, shame is where the enemy lives. He is *"the accuser of the brethren"* (Revelation 12:10). He thrives in hiddenness and echoes the same lie he whispered in Eden: "Did

God really say…?" His strategy hasn't changed. He wants to strip you of your confidence in Christ and keep you covered in fig leaves of pride, perfection, and false humility. But Psalm 34:5 declares, *"Those who look to him are radiant; their faces are never covered with shame."* We were never meant to live in hiding. We were meant to live in the light. *"Where the Spirit of the Lord is, there is freedom"* (2 Corinthians 3:17 NLT). That freedom invites you to take off the mask, lay down the armor, and let grace reach the parts you've been trying to protect.

You don't have to protect yourself anymore. You don't have to prove your worth. The blood already paid for your access. The Spirit already unlocked the door, and Father already knows everything, and He still calls you His. So, trade your pride for peace. Lay down your shame for sonship. Let the false humility fall and let true humility rise. Not the kind that hides, but the kind that lifts its eyes to Heaven and says, "Lord, use me for Your glory."

Already Becoming

This final chapter of the healing part of the book is not an altar call to effort, but an invitation to rest. Not in your performance, but in His promise. It is the kind of grace that meets you in the middle of the mess. Before you clean it up, before you get it right, and before you even know what healing is supposed to look like. It's the kind that strips away shame, perfectionism, and fear so that healing can go deeper and last longer.

Healing didn't look like a spotlight moment. It looked like counseling sessions where I could barely get the words out. It looked like prayers that had no language, just groans and tears. It looked like pages in my journal stained with the ink of shame being poured out. It looked like conversations with my husband where, for the first time, I didn't flinch when I was seen. I didn't run from love. I received it. And in that receiving, I came to the truth: This was not my fault. This was not my identity. This was part of my story, but not the whole of it.

We do not have to strive to become what God has already declared. When a woman becomes a wife, she doesn't have to strive to be one. She simply is. When a mother gives birth or adopts, she doesn't have to work to be a mother; she already is one. The title does not require striving. It requires resting in the truth of what already exists. So, it is with you. You don't have to become worthy of being loved. You don't have to perform to be chosen. You already are. God created you with everything you would need for everything you would face.

Identity begins with rest, not with work. It begins with truth, not trauma, and it is sustained by grace, not grit. You are not becoming in the sense of striving. You are becoming in the sense of unveiling. You are already becoming who He said you are, and you don't have to hustle for what heaven already handed you. Jesus showed His scars to Thomas as proof, not that He was still bleeding, but that He had been healed. The scars weren't hidden; they were revealed. So, it is with us that our scars do not disqualify us; they testify to a Savior who heals. Isaiah 53:5 reminds us, *"By His wounds we are healed."* John 20:27 tells us Jesus said, *"Put your finger here… reach out your hand and put it into my side."* The marks remained as symbols of resurrection. Revelation 12:11 says we overcome *"by the blood of the Lamb and the word of our testimony."* You are not just healing. You are becoming, and in Christ, you are already enough.

You are already celebrated

Stop waiting to be celebrated by people who are too distracted. Their eyes may be fixed on their own fields, but that doesn't change the truth that God has already laid His hand on yours. *"Before I formed you in the womb I knew you, before you were born, I set you apart"* (Jeremiah 1:5, NLT). His affirmation doesn't require applause. Some people are simply tending to the gardens God gave them: their families, their ministries, their assignments. It's not because they overlooked you, but because Heaven has stirred them to water what they've been entrusted with. *"Each of you should use whatever gift you have received to serve others, as faithful stewards of God's grace"* (1 Peter 4:10, NLT). Their silence isn't always rejection; sometimes it's obedience.

Don't measure your value by whether someone sees your growth. God sees in secret and rewards openly (Matthew 6:4). While you're waiting to be celebrated, He's calling you to pick up your own watering can and steward what He's planted in you. You're not responsible for someone else's garden, just your own. *"So neither the one who plants nor the one who waters is anything, but only God, who makes things grow"* (1 Corinthians 3:7, NLT). If you abandon your assignment to chase affirmation, you risk forfeiting the harvest He promised.

There are others who are not Kingdom-minded at all. They've traded in the gospel for the American dream by pursuing platforms and prosperity with religious language but empty fruit. Jesus warned of this in Matthew 7:21–23: *"Not everyone who calls out to me, 'Lord! Lord!' will enter the Kingdom of Heaven… Only those who actually do the will of my Father in heaven will enter."* The gospel was never about gaining fame or fortune it was about laying down your life. Jesus said plainly, *"If anyone wants to follow me, he must deny himself, take up his cross daily, and follow me"* (Luke 9:23, NLT). There is no crown without a cross. The American dream may promise ease, but the gospel promises eternal reward through daily surrender.

Stop shrinking, waiting for someone else to affirm what Heaven already announced. *"The Lord your God is with you, the Mighty Warrior who saves. He will take great delight in you… He will rejoice over you with singing"* (Zephaniah 3:17,

NLT). Stop abandoning your garden because no one is clapping. God already called it good (Genesis 1:31) and stop chasing dreams that weren't birthed in the Spirit. *"Delight yourself in the Lord, and He will give you the desires of your heart"* (Psalm 37:4, NLT). Not the desires shaped by culture, but the ones transformed in His presence. Let the applause of Heaven be enough and the joy of the Lord be your strength (Nehemiah 8:10). Water your garden. Sow in tears if you must but know you will reap in joy (Psalm 126:5). There is fruit in you that will feed nations, and there is a God who already sees it.

Refection

1. In what ways have you been waiting on others to heal a wound that God has given you the authority to confront?

2. Are you delaying obedience or joy because you're still waiting for applause from people God never assigned to your journey?

3. What lies have you agreed with about yourself that God never said, and how have those lies shaped your choices?

4. Where have you mistaken familiarity for safety, and how might God be calling you out of what's known and into what's holy?

5. What painful truth have you been avoiding, and what would it look like to bring that into the light with God?

6. Where in your life are you striving to become something that God has already declared you to be?

Prophetic Declaration – The Unburdened Heart

I declare in the name of Jesus that I am no longer bound by perfectionism, fear, or shame. Every burden I have carried that did not come from God is being lifted now. I trade anxiety for peace, pressure for promise, and striving for rest.

I am not defined by what I have gone through. My scars do not disqualify me; they testify that I am healed by the blood of the Lamb. I no longer hide behind false strength, but I live in the freedom of honesty before God and His people.

I declare that fear has no power over me. The spirit of fear is broken, and I walk in power, love, and a sound mind. I am not waiting to be celebrated by man, because Heaven already rejoices over me.

I step into true humility that does not shrink back but boldly receives the grace of God. My identity is not in performance, but in His promise. I am already becoming who God says I am.

From this day forward, I live unburdened, unashamed, and unafraid. I am God's beloved, chosen, and set apart. My heart is free, my mind is sound, and my life will reveal His glory.
In Jesus' name, Amen.

Part Three: Wholeness

Walking in Freedom

Isaiah 58:11 – "You will be like a well-watered garden..."

Prayer:

Lord, You are the Master Gardener of my soul. Thank You for not just pulling up the weeds of my past but for planting something new and beautiful in their place. As I walk into this final stretch of healing, I ask for Your living water to nourish every dry and broken place within me. Make me like a well-watered garden, flourishing in Your grace, rooted in Your truth, and free to grow in the light of Your presence. Let the freedom You died to give me become the rhythm I walk in daily. I trust You to finish what You started and to carry me from healing into wholeness. In Jesus' name, Amen

Chapter 7

What Wholeness Really Looks Like

I want to start this chapter with a confession. When I first sat down to write this book, I tried to approach it the way my religious self would be proud of. I imagined myself locked away in a room fasting for 40 days, wrapped in a mantle of revelation, surrounded by angelic visitations and spiritual downloads so powerful they'd melt the pages. In my mind, that was the formula for a best-selling, heart-piercing, God-glorifying book. But God, being the kind Father that He is, refused to let me stay in that mindset. None of those things happened. I snacked while I wrote. I laughed with my kids in between paragraphs. I scrolled. And guess what? God still spoke.

He whispered between the ordinary. He met me digging in the fridge and the pantry looking for snacks. He swept me off my feet not with fire or earthquakes, but with reminders like He did for Elijah, that He often speaks in a still small voice (1 Kings 19:11-12). Over and over, He's been breaking religion and legalism in me. There's a danger in trying to follow Christ through the lens of legalism. It tricks you into believing that God's love is a reward for good behavior instead of the foundation for your freedom. Legalism says, "Do more." Jesus says, *"Come to Me"* (Matthew 11:28). Legalism is performative, and it looks holy, but it can be hollow. Jesus constantly rebuked the religious leaders of His day for this very thing: appearing righteous on the outside while neglecting justice, mercy, and faith on the inside (Matthew 23:23–28). He didn't come to reinforce the heavy burdens religion placed on people; He came to lift them.

Jesus modeled what it looked like to obey the Father, not the expectations of man. He healed on the Sabbath, dined with sinners, touched the unclean, and forgave the guilty. He chose love over law, compassion over tradition, truth over image. That example still calls us today, not to be impressive, but to be intimate with Father. Wholeness isn't reserved for those who get everything right. It's not built on the pressure of perfection but the presence of Jesus. It's the quiet, steady work of letting Him transform us from the inside out. It's brick upon brick and discipline by discipline. Forming a beautiful marriage between your spirit and the Spirit of God, between your healed heart and the people God calls you to love. It looks like spiritual disciplines that nourish you, boundaries that protect you, relationships that sharpen you, rest that grounds you, and intentional living that keeps you focused. This chapter is about that kind of wholeness. Holy and real, not loud and flashy.

Spiritual Disciplines: Foundations, Not Formulas

Spiritual disciplines are not performance metrics for God's approval. They are invitations into deeper communion with Him. For so long, I thought fasting, prayer, and studying were the prerequisites for His voice, as if the Spirit of the living God could be manipulated by my consistency. But the truth is, He meets us in the middle of our busy schedules. The goal of discipline is not checking a task off your checklist or control; it's connection. Connection is where transformation happens. Paul tells Timothy to *"train yourself to be godly"* (1 Timothy 4:7 NLT), but this training doesn't happen in a vacuum. It happens in kitchens, in car lines, during morning runs or walks, during quiet early mornings, or late-night tears. It happens when you open your Bible with expectation, even if you're still wiping sleep from your eyes. God honors the heart, not just the habit.

Spiritual disciplines are akin to bricks and deep roots. These bricks are not the kind that build towers of pride, but the kind that build strong foundations. Deep roots that keep you grounded when the storms of life come. Jesus, fully God and fully man, often withdrew to quiet places to pray (Luke 5:16), not to escape the people, but to be refilled for them. We cannot pour from an empty vessel. We cannot offer to others what we haven't first received from Father. When we attempt to conjure up the Spirit of God from an undisciplined life, as if we could manipulate His presence through emotionalism or performance, it reveals a deeper deception of ourselves. You can speak in tongues and still be empty. You can lead worship and still be dry. You can post scriptures on social media and still not be surrendered. God isn't impressed by how we package our presence before Him; He desires surrender so that He can pour Himself in.

Prayer, fasting, study, worship, these are not boxes to check or something will go terribly wrong, no, they are lifelines. These disciplines break our soul (our will, mind, and emotions) and align our spirit with the will of Father and reassure our true identity. Trying to give out when you haven't been filled is like offering someone water from a broken cup. Discipline without intimacy leads to burnout, and revelation without repentance leads to pride. It's just a simple act and not a relationship. Just like Paul writes in 2 Timothy 3:5 KJV, *"Having a form of godliness, but denying the power thereof..."*. If you don't consistently allow God to fill you, your ministry, parenting, relationships, and creativity will all suffer and become performative. But when you learn to prioritize presence over productivity, you shift from striving to abiding, and when you abide, fruit grows naturally (John 15:5).

Paul's instruction to Timothy was to *"train yourself to be godly"* (1 Timothy 4:7 NLT), not for applause, but for alignment. Discipline grounded in love becomes worship. Wholeness isn't about how often you do the disciplines but how deeply they root you in Christ. If you've struggled with consistency, grace still calls you closer. So do not give up. If you've felt spiritually dry, discipline can dig the well again. When you stop striving and start abiding, you'll realize that even in your weakness, God is always faithful to meet you where you are.

Setting Boundaries: The Ministry of "No!"

Boundaries are not walls to keep people out; they are gates that protect what God has planted in you. Gardening has become one of my favorite things to do. I love planting a seed and watching the seedlings grow and then watching the fruit of the tree flourish. Nothing is more rewarding and peaceful, honestly. As the seed is transformed, its roots deepen, and its fruit begins to flourish. A wise gardener would purchase some sort of netting or covering to keep the fruit from being eaten by the animals. These boundaries are not just about who you say no to, but what you're saying yes to. Putting nets up tells the animals you cannot have this because this is preserved for my family. For too long, many of us were taught that love meant overextending ourselves, giving until we were depleted, and saying yes so that we wouldn't be seen as selfish. But healthy love, God's kind of love, includes limits in God's timing. Even Jesus had boundaries. He didn't heal everyone in every city. He didn't answer every question from the Pharisees. He often slipped away to be alone (Mark 1:35), not because He didn't care, but because He was aligned with the Father's timing and priorities. If Jesus, who was perfect, set boundaries, how much more should we, who are still being perfected?

Saying "no" isn't unchristian; it's wise. Proverbs 4:23 says, "Guard your heart above all else, for it determines the course of your life." That means everything can't have access to you. Not every invitation deserves a yes, not every phone call deserves a callback, not every emergency is your emergency, and not every relationship should be renewed just because time has passed. Boundaries are how you steward your soul.

There was a time I thought setting boundaries meant I lacked compassion or grace and that I had to be someone who lived as a sacrifice, no matter how much it hurt me, my marriage, my children, or my extended relationships. But what I've learned is that God's grace also gives you the wisdom to stop bleeding for people who are not assigned to your healing. Jesus bled once, for all. You don't have to crucify yourself daily for the sake of everyone else's comfort. Wholeness means learning how to love others without losing yourself. It's understanding that "no" is not a rejection, it's a form of protection. It's also a form of worship when your "no" helps you remain obedient to the pace, peace, and priorities God has for your life. Boundaries don't close your heart; they clarify your call.

Nurturing Healthy Relationships: Healing in Community

Wholeness was never meant to be a solo journey. From the beginning, God said, "It is not good for man to be alone" (Genesis 2:18). While that verse is often applied to marriage, the principle goes deeper: we were created for connection, covenant and community. Healing may begin in private, but it is sustained in relationships and not just any relationships healthy ones.

Unhealthy relationships drain what God is trying to develop. They keep you locked in cycles of comparison, compromise, and confusion. But healthy relationships, the kind rooted in truth, accountability, grace, and mutual growth remind you who you are in Christ, especially when you forget. Proverbs 27:17 says, "As iron sharpens iron, so a friend sharpens a friend." Sharpening isn't always comfortable, but it is necessary. The right people will call you up, not just call you out. They will love you enough to confront the lies the enemy has planted throughout your life that you believe about yourself.

As God has healed my heart, He's also healed the way I relate to people. I used to bond through brokenness, drawing close to those who mirrored my dysfunction or made me feel needed. But healing required me to break those soul ties and develop new patterns of connection. I had to learn that loyalty isn't measured by longevity, and closeness isn't the same as covenant. Some people were familiar but not fruitful. Others were seasonal but not safe. God began teaching me to choose relationships based on alignment, not just attachment.

I remember having a conversation with a friend during a season when I was deeply hurt over someone who had suddenly stopped speaking to me. I couldn't understand why. I wasn't sure if I had hurt her, and I carried the guilt like a weight I couldn't put down. What grieved me most was not just the loss of connection, but the fear that somehow, I had disrupted her ability to connect with others and even with God. I voiced this to my friend, and her response was like cold water to my burning anxiety: "You're delusional," she said, not in harshness, but in truth. "You cannot control how someone feels or how they connect with others, especially not how they connect with God." She reminded me, firmly and graciously, that I cannot fix people and, in that moment, after I chose to hear God through her, the heavy burden was lifted.

I realized that my desire to shrink myself to make room for that person in my life wasn't humility. It was fear disguised as love. I wasn't trying to be Christlike; I was trying not to be abandoned. I was trying to prove my worth by enduring pain, but that's not wholeness, that's bondage. That is a cycle that I found in my life, time after time, because of early sexual abuse. I tend to protect the perpetrator by keeping quiet, but it's the quietness that eats away at the soul. Healthy relationships don't require self-erasure. They don't ask you to bleed so someone else can feel better. They call you to truth, not trauma. Healthy relationships require honesty, boundaries, and grace. You don't have to earn your place in someone's life when love is real and mutual. And you don't have to beg to be understood when you're walking with people who are led by the Spirit.

Here's the complexity of relationships: if you've been hurt in the community, you cannot let the pain from someone else isolate you. Healing happens when we risk connection again with wisdom. James 5:16 reminds us, "Confess your sins to each other and pray for each other so that you may be healed." Relationships are sustained where honesty, prayer, and love flow freely. You were never meant to grow alone. Even Jesus surrounded Himself with disciples. Peter denied Him, He knew Judas would betray Him, but He didn't stop investing in those around Him. Why? Because connection is part of the call. Wholeness means learning how to recognize safe people, build from a place of healing, and release the relationships that were never meant to go with you into your next season.

Resting: The Rebellion Against Performance

Rest is more than sleep; it's trust and it's worship. It is warfare against the lie that says, "You are only as valuable as what you can produce." In a world that glorifies hustle, God calls us to Sabbath, not just a day, but a posture. A rhythm of grace that refuses to bow to burnout. When you've been wounded, especially by rejection or abandonment, it can feel safer to stay busy. Busyness becomes a barrier to intimacy with God and with yourself. You perform, you serve, you strive not because you're fulfilled, but because you're afraid to be still. Stillness invites you to feel, to remember, to grieve, to listen, and for many of us, stillness exposes just how exhausted we really are.

Wholeness requires rest. Hebrews 4:9–10 (NLT) says, "So there is a special rest still waiting for the people of God. For all who have entered God's rest have rested from their labors, just as God did after creating the world." That rest isn't just for Heaven; it's for now. It's for those who trust that God is sovereign enough to keep things moving even when we are not. That His power is not diminished by our pause. I used to think rest was for when the work was done. But with God, rest is what equips you to do the work well. It is a sacred act of defiance against the enemy's tactics of anxiety, perfectionism, and overcommitment. When you rest, you remind your soul that God doesn't need your hustle; He desires your heart.

Recently, I found myself on a long road trip, riding. I was not in the driver's seat, not even in the passenger seat, but in the back. That may seem like a small thing, but for someone who likes to control the pace, the playlist, the pit stops, and the conversation, it was uncomfortable. I couldn't choose how fast we were going. I couldn't weigh in on where we'd eat or what was playing on the radio. I had no control, and it was in that place of stillness that the Holy Spirit whispered: This is the lesson.

Rest is the enemy of control and control is often the mask we wear to avoid confronting our lack of trust and the desire to perform. There's a breaking that happens in that space. A holy kind of discomfort where your desire to manage everything and desire to please gets exposed. But there's also oil there. Oil that only comes through the agony and anxiety of letting go. When you're not steering the journey, you have no choice but to trust the One who is.

So, I stopped and asked, "God, what are You putting Your finger on? Why do I feel the need to control everything? And why is it so hard to just rest?" He didn't respond with lightning. He responded with clarity: Because you've mistaken control for safety, and you've confused movement with progress. Let Me show you another way.

You don't have to strive to be what you already are. Just like a wife doesn't strive to be a wife once she is married, or a mother doesn't strive to be a mother once she has a child, your identity in Christ is secure. Rest anchors you in that truth. It reminds you that you are already seated in heavenly places (Ephesians 2:6), already chosen, already loved, already enough.

Wholeness doesn't happen in overdrive. It happens in surrender and surrender begins with rest.

Living Intentionally: Daily Choices That Shape Eternal Impact

"Wholeness is not a destination, it's a posture." Apostle Shari Eddington. Wholeness is intentionally built daily. It isn't built in a day. Nor is it the result of one mountaintop moment or a weekend conference. It's the fruit of resolve and of small, intentional, Spirit-led decisions made over and over again. To live intentionally means you no longer drift through life reacting to what happens. You live on purpose, with purpose, and for God's purposes.

When healing begins to take root, you start to realize that your time, your thoughts, your relationships, and your habits are most important. You can no longer afford to live on autopilot. Ephesians 5:15–17 (NLT) says, *"So be careful how you live. Don't live like fools, but like those who are wise. Make the most of every opportunity in these evil days. Don't act thoughtlessly but understand what the Lord wants you to do."* That's the call to intentionality to live with eyes open and heart surrendered.

Intentional living means asking the Holy Spirit to help you pause before you respond, pray before you assume, and surrender before you strive. It means making space for what truly matters and being willing to prune what doesn't. It's choosing purpose over popularity, and obedience over opportunity.

There was a time when I thought purpose had to be loud. I had to mount platforms, gain thousands of followers, and there had to be applause because that meant I hit the target. But healing taught me that God's will is often fulfilled in obscurity. Purpose and intentionality often look like responding to your child with patience, honoring your body with care, showing up to therapy, reading your Bible before picking up your phone, forgiving quickly, and asking hard questions when needed. It's not glamorous, but it is powerful. It is purpose.

Living intentionally doesn't mean every day will feel deep or profound. It means you trust that God is in the details. He's in your Monday morning, your messy kitchen, your tired prayers, your honest yes, and your brave no. When you live intentionally, you learn to steward both the quiet and the crowded, both the joy and the stretching, because every moment becomes an offering.

Intentional wholeness isn't passive. It's active surrender. It's choosing to walk in alignment with God's heart even when it's inconvenient, unpopular, or unseen. It's building a life that doesn't just look healed but is healed, intentionally and with purpose.

Reflection and Activation

- What areas of your spiritual life have been more about performance than connection? Where is God inviting you to meet with Him in simple, quiet, and ordinary moments?

- Where have you struggled to say "no," and what fear might be hiding beneath that struggle? How could setting healthy boundaries be a form of obedience and protection?

- Are there relationships you've been trying to fix or maintain at the cost of your peace? Who in your life sharpens you in Christ, and who may need to be released in this season of healing?

- What does your current rhythm of life reveal about your trust in God? Are you allowing yourself to rest, or are you striving to earn what you already have in Him?

- What parts of your daily life feel like they're on autopilot? How can you invite the Holy Spirit into your decisions so that you live with greater intention and alignment?

Prophetic Declaration of Wholeness

I declare that I am whole in Christ, not by performance, but by His presence. I am no longer bound by legalism, perfectionism, or fear, for Jesus has set me free to abide in His love. My spirit is rooted in Him, my boundaries are guarded by His wisdom, my relationships are healed by His truth, my rest is secured in His sovereignty, and my days are ordered with divine intention.

I choose connection over control, obedience over opportunity, and intimacy over image. I will not bleed for what God has not assigned me to carry, nor will I strive to earn what I already am. I am chosen, loved, and complete in Him. I declare that my wholeness is rising, brick by brick, breath by breath, moment by moment, as I surrender to the steady hand of the Father.

From this day forward, I walk in alignment with heaven's rhythm; anchored, guarded, and overflowing with grace. I am whole, I am free, and I am becoming all that God has called me to be.

Chapter 8

Identity Reclaimed

I didn't know I was in an identity overhaul until everything familiar began to unravel. I thought I knew who I was, what I wanted, what I wanted my life to look like, although on the inside, I was miserable and felt like I was trapped, fighting to get out. It was like, I knew there was more to get to, but didn't quite know how to get there. I always say that God literally kicked me out of an old place and into healing. It was a painfully freeing experience. Healing had begun but so had the breaking. I was walking through abandonment, rejection, and discovery all at once. God, in His complexity, was stripping away everything I had accepted as true about myself that wasn't aligned with who He said I was. It was holy and it was hard. It felt like being stretched across a tightrope, between who I had become to survive and who I was being invited to become to thrive.

One day stands out. I was sitting in a meeting, and the topic was personality types: introvert, extrovert, ambivert, and all the other "verts." I remember feeling confident that I knew exactly where I landed: introvert, all the way. I had worn that label for years. I'd been told I was shy, quiet, and withdrawn, and I believed it. I told myself I enjoyed being alone and, in some ways, that was true and still is, but it wasn't the whole truth. What I hadn't yet realized was that my so-called "introversion" was rooted in fear. Fear of rejection, fear of being misunderstood, fear of doing too much or saying too much, and making someone upset. Hiding had become a coping mechanism, not a personality trait. Silence became my safety. Isolation became my armor.

God was not letting me hide anymore. That day, right in the middle of that meeting, my then pastor and a co-worker called me out in love but boldly. "You're not an introvert," they said. "Look at how you gather people. Look at the bright colors you wear, the way you make people feel seen and at home. You don't shrink back. You make room and you do it naturally." I was appalled. Surely, they were talking about someone else. But something about their words cracked something open inside of me. All those things were true. I'd always assumed staying in the background was just who I was. In the moments to come, I would realize it wasn't identity, it was injury. Somewhere along the way, the enemy had whispered a lie, and I'd agreed with it. I mistook my trauma response for personality. I confused self-protection with self-awareness. I just didn't know.

That day marked the beginning of a new kind of healing. One that didn't just soothe the wounds but began to speak truth to the roots. It was the first time I gave myself permission to explore who I was beyond the labels I had worn for survival. I started to love people fiercely without losing myself. I embraced my boldness with boundaries. I stopped apologizing for being vibrant and alive. While I haven't fully conquered the fear of speaking boldly, I'm no longer mute. I'm no longer hiding.

This chapter is for the ones who've been mislabeled. For the ones who've worn shame like a second skin and called it personality. For the ones who've been told what they're not for so long that they don't know who they are. You are not what you went through. You are not what they labeled you. You are who God says you are.

You are Beloved. You are Called. You are Whole. Reclaim your identity.

Beloved: Reclaiming the Truth That You Are Loved

Identity doesn't begin at adulthood. It doesn't begin in childhood either. It begins in the womb. God declared through the prophet Jeremiah, *"Before I formed you in the womb, I knew you. Before you were born, I set you apart"* (Jeremiah 1:5

NLT). Spiritually, our identity is rooted in God's design and His foreknowledge. But naturally and physically, we are also being shaped by our environment, even in the womb. Science affirms what Scripture has long declared: that formation is both biological and generational.

Psychologist and trauma expert Dr. Gabor Maté explains it this way: "We don't begin life when we're born. Our emotional and physiological patterns begin in utero, shaped by our mother's stress levels, emotional state, and even the unhealed pain of generations before her." When we are being formed in the womb, we are not just receiving DNA. We are receiving emotional residue. We carry the joys and the traumas of our mother, and even the inherited patterns of those who came before us. The Bible speaks to this generational inheritance, too. In Exodus 34:7, God says He *"lays the sins of the parents upon their children and grandchildren; the entire family is affected— even children in the third and fourth generations."* In some cases, patterns extend even further: *"No one born of a forbidden union may enter the assembly of the Lord; even to the tenth generation..."* (Deuteronomy 23:2 ESV). While the context is different, the principle stands: generational effects are real and long-lasting.

So, from the beginning, our identity has been under siege. Our souls are shaped before we can speak. Our first cries come into a world already whispering messages about who we are and how we should be. And while God's voice was the first to speak our name in love, the enemy is quick to follow, planting lies as early and as often as he can.

Let's face it, almost from the moment we're born, we are groomed to perform. As babies, we are celebrated for doing something cute, funny, or clever, and often corrected or scolded when we misstep. Over time, these conditions lead us to believe that love must be earned. And that's where the enemy begins his campaign of distortion. He is, after all, a liar and the father of lies (John 8:44). He plants seeds of deception, hoping they will grow into false identities:

- "You're too much."
- "You're not enough."
- "You have to earn love."
- "You're invisible."
- "You're a mistake."
- "You'll always be second."
- "You're hard to love."
- "If people really knew you, they'd leave."
- "You're only valuable when you're useful."
- "If you stay quiet, you'll stay safe."
- "Your worth is in your looks, talents, or achievements."
- "You're unlovable because of what you did or what was done to you."

Each of these lies comes to steal, kill, and destroy your sense of belovedness. John 10:10 warns us plainly: *"The thief's purpose is to steal and kill and destroy. My purpose is to give them a rich and satisfying life."* The enemy comes to steal your joy, kill your confidence, and destroy your identity, but Jesus comes to restore it all.

And here's what God says instead:

- "You are fearfully and wonderfully made." (Psalm 139:14)
- "You are the apple of His eye." (Zechariah 2:8)
- "You are precious in His sight." (Isaiah 43:4)
- "You are chosen." (1 Peter 2:9)
- "You are called by name." (Isaiah 43:1)
- "You are loved with an everlasting love." (Jeremiah 31:3)
- "You are God's masterpiece." (Ephesians 2:10)
- "You are adopted into His family." (Romans 8:15)
- "You are not forsaken." (Deuteronomy 31:6)
- "You are redeemed and forgiven." (Colossians 1:13–14)

The Cross rewrites every false narrative. Jesus didn't die for a version of you that has it all together. He died for the real, raw, and wounded you. The little girl or little boy in you who was made to believe they weren't enough. When you receive salvation, the blood that He shed doesn't just wash away your sins; it severs the power of generational iniquity. It blots out transgressions and gives Christ full authority to rewrite your spiritual DNA back to Heaven's original design. In that moment, you are given the power to renounce every generational curse and denounce every lie that has followed your bloodline. What once ran in your family can now run out. You are not bound to repeat cycles. You are free to walk in the truth of who you are in Him. Reclaiming your identity starts with receiving love, not earning it.

You are chosen, cherished, and pursued. God doesn't love from a distance. He loves in proximity. Romans 8:38–39 declares that, *"nothing can separate you from that love."* Not your past, not your mistakes, not even your doubts. You are fully known and still fully loved. Let that truth confront every lie that says you are unworthy. Healing begins where love is received without fear, because *"There is no fear in love; but perfect love casteth out fear..."* (1 John 4:18 KJV).

Called: Reclaiming the Truth That You Have Purpose

You are not an afterthought. You are appointed and anointed. Being called doesn't begin when people recognize you; it begins when God speaks over you. "Before I formed you in the womb, I knew you. Before you were born, I set you apart." (Jeremiah 1:5 NLT) Pain often tells us that we're disqualified, but God doesn't revoke purpose because of brokenness. He redeems it. Thank you, God! Excuse me while I give God a shout of praise! He is the Redeemer of all things, including your call.

The Hebrew word for redeemer is "go'el" (גֹּאֵל), which literally means kinsman redeemer or one who rescues or recovers by paying a price. In ancient Israel, a go'el was a close relative who had the legal right and responsibility to restore what was lost. They would redeem property, defend bloodlines, and even marry a widowed woman to keep a family name alive. The go'el didn't just save, they restored. They put things back in order.

So, when we call Jesus our Redeemer, we're not just saying He saved us; we're saying He restored us. He stepped into our broken lineage and claimed us as His own. He paid the price with His blood to bring us back into right standing, not just with God, but with our calling, our identity, and our destiny. Isaiah 43:1 says, *"Fear not, for I have redeemed you; I have called you by name; you are mine."* Redemption isn't just a theological term; it's a personal testimony.

To the Church, Christ as our Redeemer means we are not slaves to sin, cycles, or shame. We have been bought back from the grip of death. Individually, it means that even if your story includes detours, delays, and disasters, none of it disqualifies you. Why? Because your Go'el has the final say. The One who knows your family history and every flaw still chose you, still called you, and still covered you. He doesn't waste anything, not even your wounds.

He called Moses a deliverer while he was still stuttering in the wilderness. Even after Moses repeatedly said he couldn't do it, God never withdrew the assignment. He called David king while he was still a teenage shepherd, smelling like sheep, and then sent him back to the field to wait until the timing aligned with the anointing. He called Mary "highly favored" while she was still unknown, unmarried, and at risk of being stoned for carrying a child that didn't yet make sense to those around her.

And then there's Peter.

Peter, the loud, impulsive, passionate disciple who said the right things one moment and the completely wrong things the next. The same Peter who stepped out of the boat to walk on water and then sank when fear overtook his faith. The same Peter who cut off a man's ear trying to defend Jesus, but later denied even knowing Him, not once, but three times. If failure disqualified someone from being used by God, Peter should've been the first to be benched. Yet, after the resurrection, Jesus didn't shame Peter, He reinstated him. He cooked him breakfast and asked, not for an apology, but for love: *"Peter, do you love me?"* (John 21). After each confession of love, Jesus said, *"Then feed my sheep."*

This is redemption in action. This is what it means to be called not because you got it all right, but because God already saw your future and chose you anyway. He called Peter a rock even when he was still shaky. He called him the ekklesia, the foundation for the future church, knowing full well Peter would fall. And still, He never changed His mind. Your calling is not fragile or up for public affirmation; it's based on divine assignment. To reclaim your identity is to agree with Heaven about why you were born. You are not wandering; you are sent.

You are not random; you are positioned. Even your pain is being repurposed. Romans 8:28 assures us that God works all things together for good to them who love Him and are called according to His purpose. So, step out of hiding. Say yes again. You are still called.

Whole: Reclaiming the Truth That You Are Not Broken Beyond Repair

Wholeness doesn't mean perfection but restoration. It means Shalom: nothing missing and nothing lacking. The world will tell you that you are too damaged, too far gone, too much to fix. But Isaiah 61 reveals Jesus as the One who binds up the brokenhearted and gives beauty for ashes. Healing isn't surface level. It's a deep, Spirit-led transformation. It reaches the parts of us we've buried, ignored, or numbed. Wholeness is not something you achieve. It's something you receive through surrender. *"Therefore, if anyone is in Christ, he is a new creation. The old has passed away. Behold, the new has come."* (2 Corinthians 5:17 ESV) That includes new mindsets, new identity, and new possibilities.

Wholeness allows you to stop striving to fix yourself and instead yield to the One who already paid for your healing. You may have been wounded, but you are not your wounds. You are not your diagnosis, your history, or your trauma. You are whole in Christ. Your identity is not wishful thinking. It's a divine reality waiting to be reclaimed.

Could it be, as Apostle Shari Eddington once revealed, that wholeness is not a destination but a living posture? That through Jesus Christ, we don't live striving for wholeness, but we live from it? That it's not a finish line but a mindset, a day-by-day agreement that what Christ did on the cross is enough? If that revelation is true, then wholeness becomes the lens through which we make decisions, forgive deeply, love fully, and rest freely. It is how we navigate life, not with perfection, but with peace. Reclaiming the Shalom of God is not only for you. It is generational. It is for your children, and your children's children, and for every generation that follows. When you reclaim wholeness, you interrupt the enemy's plan to annihilate your bloodline. You break the patterns and silence the voices that said, "This is just how it will always be." No. Shalom is not a destination. It is a consistent determination that proclaims, "Jesus is Lord over my life and over my lineage." It's a banner that waves over you when you're too tired to fight. It's the flag of Heaven raised in defiance against generational dysfunction and despair.

Yahweh Nissi (The Lord is my Banner, Exodus 17:15) is your covering in the battle. His banner doesn't fade in storms. His banner doesn't fall when you stumble. His banner remains. Reclaiming Shalom is not just recovery. It's an inheritance. It is your birthright as a son or daughter of the Most High. You don't have to earn it. You just have to receive it and walk in it.

So, lift your head. Straighten your crown. The Lord your God is restoring all things, including your wholeness.

Reflection

1. What labels have you worn that were actually rooted in fear, trauma, or survival rather than truth?

2. When you think back to your childhood, what messages (spoken or unspoken) shaped how you saw yourself?

3. Which lies from the enemy have you unconsciously agreed with (e.g., "I'm not enough," "I have to earn love")?

4. How has God already shown you glimpses of your true identity through other people's words, affirmations, or your own experiences?

5. What generational patterns or family narratives do you feel God is inviting you to break in this season?

6. How does knowing you are *Beloved* shift the way you view yourself today?

7. Where in your life have you mistaken injury for identity?

8. What does reclaiming wholeness look like in practical steps for you right now?

Prophetic Declaration of Wholeness

I decree and declare that my identity is not defined by trauma, labels, or lies. Every false name spoken over me is broken by the blood of Jesus. I reclaim the truth that I am beloved, chosen, and whole. I walk boldly in my divine purpose, knowing that I am not an accident or an afterthought. Generational cycles are severed, and Heaven's design for my life is restored. I live from wholeness, not striving for it, because Christ has already made me new. From this day forward, I refuse to hide, shrink, or apologize for who God created me to be. I rise in my true identity as a child of God; fully loved, fully called, and fully whole.

Chapter 9

Maintaining the life, you've built

Healing doesn't end at the altar. It doesn't conclude with a tearful prayer, a breakthrough moment, or even the final page of a book. Healing must be maintained. It is a daily choice to guard what God has restored. Just like a wound that once required stitches must still be protected from re-injury, your healing must be stewarded with wisdom, intentionality, and spiritual discipline. Deliverance may happen in a moment, but discipleship is what keeps it. The enemy does not give up easily. He constantly accuses us of something before Father. Jesus warned us in Luke 11:24-26 that unguarded deliverance can invite an even worse return. This is not said to scare you but to sober you. We don't drift into wholeness; we walk there, step by step, choosing truth over lies, light over darkness, and grace over guilt.

Maintenance isn't about fear; it's about partnership. God has done the healing, but we are called to walk it out. Just as the Israelites had to take possession of the land God already gave them (Joshua 1:3), you must take hold of your healing. That means building boundaries, renewing your mind, staying planted in community, and confronting the subtle lies that try to creep back in. It means standing firm in your identity, even when your feelings falter. You may still feel the echo of old patterns, but now you have the tools, the truth, and the authority to silence them. This chapter will remind you that freedom is not a one-time event; it's a lifestyle, and you are not maintaining it alone. The Holy Spirit is your Helper, your Defender, and your Guide as you keep walking in wholeness.

When Old Wounds Try to Resurface: The Battle for Your Mind, Your Identity, and Your Bloodline

If you didn't know it, just by surviving birth, you've already been in a fight for life your entire life. You've been haunted by a spiritual psycho every single day, one whose only goal is to take you out. Jesus didn't leave us ignorant of this reality. In John 10:10, He warned, "The thief does not come except to steal, and to kill, and to destroy. But I have come that they may have life, and that they may have it more abundantly." And verse 1 of that same chapter tells us that this thief tries to enter the sheepfold another way, which in the

Greek *eiserchomai (ice-er'-khom-ahee)* can metaphorically mean "to enter into the mind."

The enemy doesn't always come kicking down the door. Sometimes he sneaks in through familiar thoughts, old patterns, or unhealed emotions. The Hebrew word for serpent in Genesis 3 is nāchāsh, meaning enchanter, whisperer, or spell-caster. His primary weapon isn't destruction. It's deception. He delays through distraction and destroys through delay. Have you ever felt heavy, like something was sitting on your chest, a thought you couldn't shake, a shame you couldn't name? I've felt it too. Through my healing journey, I've entered this maintenance phase more than once, and you will too. I've battled this before, but this time felt different. I turned on worship. I read Scripture. I prayed. But nothing was breaking. In the past, I would have spiraled: I must have messed up. Maybe God's mad at me. Maybe I'm not clean enough. But not this time. This time, I paused and searched deeper. I asked the Holy Spirit to show me the root, not just the symptom. I looked at my assignment. I asked, what is the enemy trying to block? I realized this wasn't about me. It was a tactic of the enemy, using old wounds as a weapon of delay.

Then there are people you'll meet, and no matter where the conversation starts, it always circles back to the same wound. They're bleeding from what happened decades ago, hemorrhaging pain that never healed. That's what happens when we eat the intoxicating fruit. Those lies, hurts, and entitlements the enemy offers us are disguised as truth. We become drunk on deception. And when you're intoxicated, you lose control of your faculties. The fruit begins to speak louder than the Father.

Healing is not the absence of memory. It's the presence of peace in the place of pain. But even after deep inner work, old wounds have a way of creeping back in, especially when we're tired, vulnerable, or stepping into new seasons. That's why spiritual alertness is vital. Paul exhorts us in Ephesians 6:10–18 to put on the full armor of God. We are not wrestling against flesh and blood but against spiritual schemes designed to make us question our healing and identity. The renewing of our minds, as Paul says in Romans 12:2, is not a one-time act. It is a daily discipline. We must build habits of prayer, Scripture meditation, and healthy boundaries that support sustained wholeness.

This is nothing new.

- Moses was intoxicated by people pleasing (Numbers 20). He was delayed in the wilderness and missed the Promised Land.

- David, enticed by lust (2 Samuel 11), saw the death of his child and trauma ripple through his house.

- Solomon was overtaken by compromise (1 Kings 11), and his legacy was fractured.

- Samson revealed his strength instead of concealing it (Judges 16) and ended his life blind and bound.

- Saul wrestled with an identity crisis and spiritual confusion until he chose death over destiny (1 Samuel 28).

- Martha missed the moment to sit at the feet of Jesus, too consumed with working for the One she could have worshiped (Luke 10).

- Judas, intoxicated by religion and riches, traded the Savior for silver and lost everything (Matthew 26).

The common thread? Each was lured by something that looked right but was intoxicating. *"There is a way that seems right to a man, but the end thereof is death."* (Proverbs 14:12) *"If then you were raised with Christ, seek those things which are above... Set your mind on things above, not on things on the earth."* (Colossians 3:1–2) *"And hath raised us up together and made us sit together in heavenly places in Christ Jesus."* (Ephesians 2:6) If you're still fighting the enemy eye to eye, you're standing too low. You cannot fight this from a low place. Your gaze is too low. Eyes up. Eyes open. You must go up. You are already seated in heavenly places. You don't need to earn your place. You just need to occupy your seat. Put on the full armor. Stay on the wall. Govern your mind, your house, and your legacy from a higher place. You are a watchman. You are a son of God. You are the planting of the Lord, a tree of righteousness. You are an heir and a joint heir. You are not powerless. You are not broken. You are called to rule from above.

So, when the old wound whispers, don't panic. Praise. Make the exchange. *"...to give them beauty for ashes, the oil of joy for mourning, the garment of praise for the spirit of heaviness..."* (Isaiah 61:3). Put on your garment of praise. Because praise isn't just a sound. It's a strategy. It resets your perspective. It lifts your eyes above the lies. It magnifies the goodness of God until you remember who you are and whose you are. Because when old wounds try to resurface, you don't deny the memory. You invite peace into the place of pain. You interrupt the spiral. You refuse the whispers. You silence the serpent. You lift your head. And you remember...You're not fighting for victory. You're fighting it.

Becoming a Vessel for Others: From Shame to Strength

God never wastes a wound. Every healed scar becomes a testimony of His power, and every victory over pain is an invitation to help someone else rise. But before we can become vessels for others, we must confront the shame that keeps us bound. For many, especially survivors of sexual assault, shame is not something they chose. It was deposited into their spirit the moment the violation occurred. It's as if the act itself makes a spiritual imprint, a silent signature that says, "You're stained." If left unchecked, that lie will keep you quiet for life.

I know that shame. I remember the first time I stood to speak. Not for my own vindication, but because I knew God would use even that for His glory. It wasn't easy. But God doesn't need perfect words. He just needs surrendered hearts. What the enemy meant for evil, God turned for good (Genesis 50:20), and not just my good. Your testimony becomes a weapon. Your resilience becomes a key that unlocks freedom in others. Shame says, "Hide." But God says, "Speak." Shame says, "You're unworthy." But God says, "You're chosen." The very thing the enemy tried to use to silence you is the thing God will use to set others free. You are not what happened to you. You are what God has healed in you. According to Genesis 12:2, we are blessed to be a blessing. That blessing includes your voice. That blessing includes your scars. When you speak, when you mentor, when you sit with another soul in silent solidarity, you are ministering deliverance. Healing transitions from internal restoration to external ministry when we let God use our story.

You don't have to shout it from the rooftops. But when God says, "Tell it," Trust that He's already prepared the ears that need to hear it. Healed people heal people. Your healing is proof that God's grace goes deeper than pain and louder than shame.

A New Beginning: Don't Miss the Moment

This section may close the book, but it opens the door to a new life. You are no longer just surviving; you are thriving. God's desire for you has never been just function, but fruitfulness. John 15:5 reminds us that abiding in Christ leads to fruit that remains. That fruit looks like peace that passes understanding, joy that the world cannot steal, and purpose that turns your pain into power. This is the celebration of your journey from brokenness to beloved, from pain to purpose, from hiding to walking boldly in freedom. Before you walk into what's next, hear the Word of the Lord: *"Forget the former things; do not dwell on the past. See, I am doing a new thing! Now it springs up; do you not perceive it?"* (Isaiah 43:18–19) God is doing a new thing in your life. Right now. Not next year. Not when everything feels perfect. Right now. Here is the warning: do not miss the moment. The children of Israel witnessed miracle after miracle yet still longed for Egypt. They were free on the outside but still enslaved in their thinking. They could not embrace the new thing God was doing because bondage had become normal to them. Let that not be your story.

The Pharisees and Sadducees missed Jesus, the very fulfillment of prophecy, walking and talking among them. The Messiah stood in their midst, offering redemption and relationship, but they were too devoted to their traditions to recognize the move of God. They clung to systems while rejecting the Savior. They missed the chance to be transformed and to help transform the world. Refuse to miss your moment to partner with what God is doing in the earth. Do not let fear of the unknown keep you tied to what is familiar. Even if you do not know the way, God does. Even if you feel unqualified, unworthy, or uncertain, God knows, and He has already gone before you. Shame, regret, or your past cannot keep you from embracing the future unless you let them. The enemy wants you stuck in cycles, but God is calling you into seasons. He is declaring over you, "Behold, I make all things new."

Let me speak to your spirit: You are not too late. You have not missed it. You are not too broken. You are right on time. There is so much more waiting for you. So much joy, peace, love, healing, and abundance. God is just getting started in your life. Your latter will be greater than your former. If you are concerned about wasted time, remember this: Jesus is the Redeemer of time. He not only restores years; He multiplies fruit. He makes up for what was stolen, delayed, or destroyed. Nothing is wasted in His hands, not even the broken pieces.

This is your invitation to move forward, not perfectly, but purposefully. Your life is a garden. Tend it. Enjoy it. Share its fruit with the world.

The best is not behind you. It is in front of you. Go get it!

Reflection

1. What daily practices help me maintain the healing and freedom God has given me?
2. Where am I still vulnerable to old wounds or patterns trying to resurface?
3. In what ways can I renew my mind daily and keep my thoughts aligned with God's truth?
4. What boundaries do I need to strengthen in this season to protect my wholeness?

5. How has shame tried to silence me, and where is God asking me to use my testimony as a vessel for others?

6. Am I living from a low place, fighting the enemy eye to eye, or am I occupying my seat in heavenly places?

7. What "new thing" is God springing up in my life right now, and how can I partner with it fully?

8. Who in my life needs the fruit of my healing, and how can I intentionally share it?

9. How am I making sure I do not miss the moment God has placed before me?

10. Where do I need to exchange ashes for beauty, mourning for joy, or heaviness for praise today?

Prophetic Declaration of Wholeness

I decree and declare that I will not just be healed. I will stay healed. I am a watchman over my mind, my house, and my legacy. I will not be lured by deception, delay, or distraction. I put on the full armor of God and occupy my seat in heavenly places. Old wounds will not define me; peace rules where pain once reigned. My scars are my testimony, and my testimony is a weapon. I will not miss my moment, for I walk in step with the Spirit. God is doing a new thing in me, and I perceive it. My latter shall be greater than my former, and my life will bear lasting fruit for His glory.

Prayer of Sealing and Sending

Father, in the name of Jesus, I thank You for every heart that has encountered this book. I ask now that You seal every truth, every revelation, every moment of conviction, comfort, and clarity. Let this not be merely pages read but a wellspring of life, a holy reference point they return to again and again as they walk out their healing journey. May this book become a trusted tool in their hands, not just for themselves, but for the generations connected to them.

Let Your light shine through them, Lord, so brightly that darkness cannot comprehend it. May the healing they have received become contagious, touching their spouses, children, friends, and communities. I ask that the principles and strategies woven throughout these chapters be etched in their hearts, minds, and spirits, never to be uprooted or forgotten. May they live out what they have learned and be living epistles of grace, restoration, and hope.

Now, God, as You heal them, send them. Send them to those who are still in the pit, those in the shadows, those who are where they once were, aching, bleeding, and silently breaking. Let their testimony be fire. Let their healing be oil. Let their love be the very reflection of You. As they go, cover them in the precious blood of Jesus. Guard their hearts in the day of battle. Remind them when it gets hard, when it gets lonely, when their own words fail, that they have a Great Intercessor who is seated at Your right hand and is always praying for them.

Let them never forget that their tears have language, that their groanings are heard in Heaven, and that their cries rise as incense before Your throne. Let them never confuse opposition with abandonment or warfare with failure. No weapon formed against them shall prosper. I declare that they are fully armored, fully equipped, and fully seated in the heavenly places with Christ Jesus.

Above all else, I pray they never forget who they are and whose they are. They are marked. They are called. They are chosen. They are covered. They are commissioned. They are deeply, irrevocably, eternally loved by Love Himself.

In Jesus' name, Amen.

Bibliography

- Nee, Watchman. *The Release of the Spirit*. New Kensington, PA: Whitaker House, 1965.
- Solomon, Torace. *The Fingerprint of God*. Self-published, 2023.
- Shari Eddington. Sermons and Teachings. Liberate Church, Dallas, TX, 2025.
- Strait, Dr. Jerry Robeson, and Dr. Carol Robeson. *Strongman's His Name… What's His Game?*. Shippensburg, PA: Whitaker House, 1996.
- **The Holy Bible, New Living Translation.** Carol Stream, IL: Tyndale House Publishers, 201

www.ingramcontent.com/pod-product-compliance
Lightning Source LLC
Chambersburg PA
CBHW060139150626
46550CB00015B/2089